The Living Festiv

C000070936

JEWISH
FESTIVALS

O M N I B U S

ROSH HASHANAH AND YOM KIPPUR,
SUCCOT AND SIMCHAT TORAH,
CHANUKAH, PASSOVER

RMEP

RELIGIOUS AND MORAL EDUCATION PRESS

Religious and Moral Education Press
An imprint of Chansitor Publications Ltd,
a wholly owned subsidiary of Hymns Ancient & Modern Ltd
St Mary's Works, St Mary's Plain
Norwich, Norfolk NR3 3BH

Individual titles first published as separate volumes in the Living
Festivals Series:

Rosh Hashanah and Yom Kippur © 1990 Frank Gent
Succot and Simchat Torah © 1987 Lynne Scholefield
Chanukah © 1983 Lynne Scholefield
Passover © 1982 Lynne Scholefield

All rights reserved. No part of this publication may be reproduced, stored in
a retrieval system, or transmitted, in any form or by any means, electronic,
electrostatic, magnetic tape, mechanical, photocopying, recording or
otherwise, without permission in writing from the publishers.

First published in this edition 1993
Reprinted 1997

ISBN   1 85175-003-7

Designed by Topics Visual Information, Exeter

Cover illustration by Debbie Tarbett

Typeset by Exe Valley Dataset

Printed in Great Britain by Redwood Books for
Chansitor Publications Ltd, Norwich

Contents

ACKNOWLEDGEMENTS
Illustrations are reproduced by courtesy of:

BBC Hulton Picture Library
Britain/Israel Public Affairs Centre and El Al
Camera Press Ltd
Sydney Harris Ltd
Jewish Programme Materials Project
Keystone Press Ltd
PJ Photography
Juliette Soester
University of London
The Warburg Institute

The words and music for the Passover songs appear by kind permission of Penguin Books Ltd, in whose book *A Passover Haggadah* they originally appeared.

Rosh Hashanah and Yom Kippur
Frank Gent

Contents

Introduction

Rosh Hashanah and Yom Kippur, the New Year and the Day of Atonement, are the most important days in the Jewish year. Synagogues are crowded with worshippers. Unlike most Jewish festivals, these are times when there are few family rituals and traditions and the synagogue becomes the most important place. A great deal of time is spent in the synagogue, especially on Yom Kippur, and it can be a deep spiritual experience. The themes and 'feel' of these services form an important part of what happens and help to give an understanding of these special days in the Jewish calendar.

1

Symbols of Rosh Hashanah: candles, wine, challah, apples and honey

Rosh Hashanah and Yom Kippur

Part 1

Rosh Hashanah

What is Rosh Hashanah?

The Hebrew words 'Rosh Hashanah' literally mean 'the head of the year' or 'the beginning of the year'. In English we would simply call it New Year's Day.

The Jewish New Year always comes in the British autumn, some time during the months of September or October. This is because the ancient Hebrews measured time by the phases of the moon rather than by the earth going round the sun. A lunar month is almost exactly four weeks and the date of Rosh Hashanah is always the first day of the Hebrew month of Tishri.

A calendar which is based on the moon (a *lunar* calendar) never fits exactly with one which is based on the sun (a *solar* calendar) and neither of them is absolutely accurate either. We have to put the solar calendar right every four years by adding an extra day in what we call 'leap' year. With the lunar calendar it is necessary to have some years of twelve months and some years of thirteen months. That is why Rosh Hashanah sometimes comes in September and sometimes in October.

Within those months it also comes on different dates each year, just like the Christian festival of Easter. And the reason for that is because Easter occurs at the same time as the Jewish festival of Passover or Pesach, another example of the Jewish calendar and the other calendar, which we call the *Gregorian* calendar, bumping into one another, as it were. (See page 75 and the book *Easter* in this series.)

Does it seem odd to have New Year's Day in the autumn? It is only a matter of habit. In England, until 1758 New Year's Day was on 25 March, near the start of spring.

The original reason for having New Year in the autumn was because it marked the end of one year and the beginning of another for farmers. Crops had been harvested. All the work of ploughing, sowing and reaping had led up to the harvest and now it would start all over again. At this point Jews found it most natural to look back over the past year before setting out on a new one. (Our word 'calendar' comes from an old Latin word *kalendae* which meant literally 'the day when all the accounts were due', when people totted up how much money they had made or lost – something farmers do after harvest but which other people might do at other times.)

When we are at school we should not find the Jewish New Year strange at all. It is very close to the beginning of what we call the academic or the school year. When teachers say, 'Next year you will be in a different class', they mean next September, not next January.

Why is Rosh Hashanah special for Jews?

For those of us who are Jews, however, Rosh Hashanah is much more than just a time for balancing the accounts in terms of money. It has great spiritual importance. We see the time as one of balancing up the accounts of our lives. Rosh Hashanah for us is a special time of repentance, of being sorry for the things which we should not have done.

A basic Jewish belief is 'You shall love your neighbour as yourself' (Leviticus 19:18). Perhaps it is easier to put this into practice if we turn it upside down, as Rabbi Hillel did nearly two thousand years ago, so that he made it read 'That which is harmful unto you, do not do unto your neighbour'.

Rosh Hashanah, then, is a time for making amends, first with friends and neighbours and then with God. It is not enough just to be sorry, though; we must do something about it. Nor does it mean that we only feel sorry once a year, but we set aside a special time of the year really to concentrate on it, so that we

Rosh Hashanah and Yom Kippur

won't keep putting it off for ever. And it is a good time of year for a fresh start, as the summer ends and autumn comes, as we settle down into a new routine and get back to normal life at school and at home after the holidays.

Other names for Rosh Hashanah

Rosh Hashanah is a time for repentance, for being sorry, as well as being the start of a new year, but there is more to it even than that. It has other names besides Rosh Hashanah and they give us clues to deeper meanings still.

First, there is the name 'Yom Hadin', which means 'The Day of Judgement'. It suggests the idea that God is also doing His accounts and judging our actions, both good and bad. For this reason God is referred to many times in prayers as 'king' – someone who sits in judgement like the kings of long ago, such as King Solomon in the Bible.

Another name sometimes used is 'Yom Hazikaron', which means 'The Day of Remembering' or 'The Day of Memorial'.

There are a lot of things to remember at Rosh Hashanah, many of them good things. We remember God's promise or covenant, given to Abraham at the time of the sacrifice of Isaac, which created the Jewish people. Jews read this story from Genesis 22 on the second morning of Rosh Hashanah. We remember also other times when God's justice has been shown in the stories of the Bible, as when He remembered Noah, or the sufferings of the Israelites in Egypt.

We also remember that in our tradition it marks the anniversary of the day God created the world. It is the world's birthday! That surely is something to be happy about.

A two-day event

Many Jewish festivals are celebrated for one day only, especially in Israel, although they may last for two days in some other places. There is a good reason for this. As we have seen, our dates depend on the phases of the moon. When the sky is clear, as it usually is in Israel, it is easy to tell when there is a new moon and a new month is beginning.

However, in ancient times, when it was cloudy it was sometimes difficult to see the new moon. Also it might take some time for Jews living far away from Jerusalem to receive confirmation that it was the new moon. For these reasons some Jewish festivals are celebrated for two days. (Muslims had exactly the same problem, as you can see if you read the book *Ramadan* in this series.)

In the case of Rosh Hashanah there is also another reason. An important part of this festival is the blowing of the shofar, but tradition forbids the playing of any musical instrument on Shabbat. By having a two-day festival, whenever Rosh Hashanah falls, it ensures that the shofar can be blown on at least one of the days.

For many Jews Rosh Hashanah may be the only time they attend a synagogue, and synagogues often have 'overflow' services in hired halls for everyone who wants to come. For a lot of Jews, going to synagogue on Rosh Hashanah is an important part of knowing who they really are and where they belong. There might be many Jewish things that they no longer believe or do, but they do not want to cut themselves off completely. For some, it is an important time to be together with friends and relations, to feel part of the community, and, at Yom Kippur, to remember and pray for parents and others who have died.

What happens at Rosh Hashanah?

The two days of Rosh Hashanah are largely taken up with services and prayers. Different Jews in different parts of the world do different things but, even so, you will find similar things taking place at this time among Jews everywhere.

The Jewish day always starts at sunset, which is why, for example, Shabbat (or Sabbath) begins on Friday evening. (See *Shabbat* in this series.) For this reason the first service for the first day of Rosh Hashanah takes place in the evening.

This is basically the same as any other evening service, but there are some extra prayers to help put us into the right 'mood'. They emphasize that God is our king and that we have sinned and want to repent and receive God's forgiveness. All the prayers

Rosh Hashanah and Yom Kippur

are chanted in Hebrew but the melody is quite different from that used on other days. This is one of the prayers which belongs to the evening service at the beginning of Rosh Hashanah.

> *Therefore, Lord our God, set such fear on every human being and such dread on all your creatures, that, in awe of You, they can worship You with humility. Then they will be a brotherhood, formed to do Your will with all their hearts. We know that the power for this comes from You and the strength and endurance that men need are in Your hands, and the fear of God is upon all Your creatures.*

In the synagogue

Next morning the congregation returns to the synagogue. As with the previous evening, the basic form of the morning service is like that of any other but with the addition of special prayers. Some of these are very complicated poems, written long ago, so that the service is much longer than usual – several hours in fact!

Once again the language used is Hebrew, although some English might be used at a Reform Jewish service. Everybody has a special prayer book called a *machzor* with a translation of every prayer to help with understanding. The prayers are chanted to the same special melody as was used at the evening service.

An important prayer is the 'Avinu malkenu' ('Our Father and King') which is a litany, or list of requests, with the theme of asking God's help and forgiveness.

> *The Avinu Malkenu*
> *Our Father, Our King, we have sinned before You.*
> *Our Father, Our King, we have no king but You.*
> *Our Father, Our King, help us for Your own sake.*
> *Our Father, Our King, grant us a new year of goodness.*
> *Our Father, Our King, keep Your children safe from disease and violence, hunger and persecution.*
> *Our Father, Our King, abolish all oppression against us.*
> *Our Father, Our King, bring true healing to our lives.*
> *Our Father, Our King, pardon us and forgive us for all our iniquities.*

Our Father, Our King, record us in the Book of Life for a decent life and livelihood.

Our Father, Our King, remember that we are but dust.

Our Father, Our King, remember us for a good life.

Our Father, Our King, record us in the Book for redemption and salvation.

Our Father, Our King, strengthen Your people Israel.

Our Father, Our King, help us to return to You in complete repentance.

Our Father, Our King, hear our voice, show us Your mercy and compassion.

Our Father, Our King, spare us, our young and our children.

Our Father, Our King, let this hour be an hour of mercy and a time You favour.

Our Father, Our King, do this because of those who are killed in Your name.

Our Father, Our King, do not send us away empty from Your presence.

Our Father, Our King, answer us with Your grace, for we lack good deeds; deal with us in charity and love and save us.

This is followed by a reading from the Torah which tells of the birth of Isaac to Abraham and Sarah when Sarah was an old woman. It is found in Genesis 21: 1-34. The story of Isaac is central to the whole story of God's covenant, or promise, to the Jewish people.

After that there is a reading from the Book of Numbers 29: 1-6, which describes very simply how Rosh Hashanah should be celebrated. It requires only that there should be 'a holy gathering', that nobody should work, just as on Shabbat, and that the shofar should be blown. It also tells of the sacrifices that had to be made in the past when the Temple stood in Jerusalem.

The third and final reading is the story of the birth of Samuel in 1 Samuel 1- 2: 10. This is read because it is very similar to the story of the birth of Isaac in the first reading. Both were a great surprise to their mothers who had given up hope of having a child.

AVINU MALKENU

Moderato

A - vi-nu mal-ke - nu ___ ha-ne-nu va-a-ne -

nu ___ a - vi-nu mal-ke-nu ha - ne - nu va - a - ne - nu ki

en ba-nu ma - a - sim ___ a - se i - ma -

nu ___ ts' - da - ka va - he - sed ___ a - se i - ma - nu

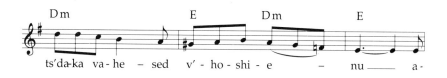

ts'da-ka va-he - sed v' - ho - shi - e ___ nu ___ a -

vi-nu mal-ke - nu ___ a - vi-nu mal ke - nu ___

The shofar

After the usual prayers for the congregation and for the Royal Family there comes the blowing of the shofar or the ram's horn. This is a very important part of the observance of Rosh Hashanah for it is commanded in the Torah. When we hear the shofar blown, the effect is very dramatic, for it is a piercing, loud noise that makes the spine tingle. To hear the shofar is a very moving experience because it transports us mentally back across the ages. It is the call to repentance. Indeed it is so important that we could add to the list of names for this festival that of 'Yom Teruah', which means simply, 'The Day of Shofar Sounding'. The ram's horn also serves as a reminder of the story of the sacrifice of Isaac in which the ram was caught in a thicket.

The blowing of the shofar comes at the end of the morning service. There are four main patterns of notes and these are blown in a fixed sequence, usually of thirty. The minister calls out the name of each note in turn for the person blowing the shofar. The notes are:

Tekiah, which is a plain note;
Shevarim – three short notes;
Teruah – nine or more very short, staccato notes;
(Shevarim-Teruah is a combination of these last two.)
Tekiah Gedolah – the final blast, a big blow that lasts as long as there is breath in the blower's lungs!

The SHOFAR Calls

The service of Musaf

Because Rosh Hashanah is a festival there is an additional (or, in Hebrew, *musaf*) service. This is because in the days of the Temple

Rosh Hashanah and Yom Kippur

Blowing the shofar

in Jerusalem an additional sacrifice was offered at festivals. Nowadays there are no Temple and no sacrifices, but additional prayers are said instead on sabbaths and festivals.

The main part of this extra service, which follows straight on from the morning service, is the 'Amidah' (Hebrew for 'standing') which is first said silently by the members of the congregation while they stand facing the Ark at the front of the synagogue. Then the Amidah is repeated aloud by the minister, but with many additional long prayers. These are on the three special themes of Rosh Hashanah:

- God as King of the universe;
- the renewing of His promises;
- the blowing of the shofar.

The shofar is then blown ten more times at the end of each of these three sections, making thirty more blasts. Each time the blowing of the shofar is followed by this prayer:

This is the birthday of the world, and one by one all creatures are questioned and examined, either as children or as servants. Take pity on us, as a father takes pity on his children. But even if we can only be Your servants, we still depend on You, until Your presence comes to us and Your judgement enlightens us, God of awe and holiness.

After the Amidah the congregation is blessed by those members who are known as *cohanim*, a plural word which simply means the priests. Cohen is a common Jewish surname, which belongs to those who are descended from the priests of the Temple in Jerusalem two thousand years ago. Then, finally, the shofar is blown again, another forty blasts, making one hundred blasts in all during the course of the service.

On the second day the services are much the same, but at the morning service the reading from the Torah is the story of the binding of Isaac from Genesis 22: 1-24. This is a strange mystical passage known as the *Akedah* (Hebrew for 'binding'). The additional reading on this second day is concerned with the idea of a kind and loving God, willing to forgive His repentant children, and is taken from Jeremiah 31:1-20.

In the home

Not everything to do with Rosh Hashanah takes place in the synagogue. It starts, in fact, in the home, when the mother of the family lights two candles before sunset to begin the festival, just like she does for Shabbat.

Before the meal on the first evening, after grace has been said, a piece of apple is dipped in honey and eaten after a blessing. Then a prayer is said requesting a good and sweet year, just like the apple and the honey we have eaten. On the second evening people usually eat a new fruit that they haven't yet eaten in the autumn such as pomegranates or figs, or even blackberries.

Just as at Shabbat, we eat a *challah*, a special kind of rich bread. However, instead of being plaited it is usually round, a bit like a giant snail's shell. It is sometimes said that this symbolizes a crown, which is appropriate because of all the prayers that are being said which describe God as a king sitting in judgement.

In the afternoon there is a lovely custom known as *Tashlich*, from the first word of the prayer which accompanies it: '... cast all the sins of the people, the house of Israel, into a place where they shall be no more remembered or visited, or ever again come to mind.' People go to a nearby river or stream or to the seashore and as they say the prayer they empty their pockets or throw breadcrumbs on the water, to symbolize being sorry for their sins.

At Rosh Hashanah we usually send all our friends and relations a greetings card with a message inside, such as 'May you be recorded in the Book of Life for a good and happy year', or the greeting may be for a sweet year, or even just 'Leshana tova!' – a good year! (See p. 22.)

During the month of Elul, which precedes Tishri, the first month of the New Year, many people visit family graves and the graves of people remembered for their example and their teaching, to remember the goodness in their lives as an inspiration to ourselves.

Overleaf: Tashlich prayers on a beach in Israel

Rosh Hashanah and Yom Kippur

Rosh Hashanah and Yom Kippur

Part 2

Yom Kippur

The days between

Rosh Hashanah, as the title of this section suggests, does not stand alone. It goes together with another important day, known as *Yom Kippur* or The Day of Atonement. This falls ten days after Rosh Hashanah, on the 10th of the Hebrew month of Tishri. These ten days are sometimes called the Days of Awe or the 'scary days', when God is making up his mind about us!

According to legend God opens a big book on Rosh Hashanah and draws up, for each of us, a sort of balance sheet on which He writes down all our good and bad deeds. We have just ten days in which to do something about our 'account' before the book is closed again on Yom Kippur.

These ten days are also known as the Days of Repentance and, even though we are busy again at work and at school, they give us a chance to put things right between us, our friends and God. For example, who, in the past year, have you made fun of, called names or rejected as friends? And what can you do about it?

Shabbat Teshuvah

The sabbath that falls during these ten days is known as Shabbat Teshuvah, or the Sabbath of Repentance. This sabbath is particularly concerned with the importance of making amends and it is the custom for the Rabbi to preach a sermon in the synagogue during the sabbath morning service to remind everyone of this.

Yom Kippur

Yom Kippur is the holiest day of the Jewish year. It begins at sunset and for the next twenty-five hours we have a complete fast of food and drink. Of course you are expected to fast only if you are thought to be old enough and in good health. Sick people or women who are pregnant are not included. If we are fasting we always have a good, sensible meal before it starts – nothing too salty, for example, in case that makes the fast even more difficult. Throughout Yom Kippur we concentrate on our souls and quite deliberately deny ourselves our usual physical comforts in order to help us be more aware of our spiritual needs. The aim of all this is atonement, an English word which simply means 'at-one-ment' or, 'being at one with', in this case God. It is a matter of getting our record straight. This is why Yom Kippur is called, in English, the Day of Atonement.

At this time of year it is important to give *tsedakah* or charity. We all have a duty to help others, but especially before Yom Kippur. As the prayer at Rosh Hashanah reminds us: 'But penitence [being sorry], prayer and charity avert the evil decree.'

Kol Nidrei

On the evening of Yom Kippur Jews assemble in the synagogue for the opening prayer of 'Kol Nidrei'. The men all wear their *tallitot* or prayer shawls, which, for the rest of the year, are worn

KOL NIDRE

Kol nid - re ve - e - sa - re va - ha - ra - me ve - ko - na - me ve - khin - nu - ye ve - kin - nu - se ushe - vu - ot

only at morning prayers. As a sign of humility leather shoes are not worn and there is a custom of wearing white, a symbol of purity. The curtain in front of the Ark, which is normally blue, is also changed for a white one.

The opening prayer of Kol Nidrei is chanted three times, to a familiar haunting melody. It is sung first in a quiet voice and then a little louder each time. This prayer has a long history and its meaning is no longer very clear but it provides a very moving opening to the service.

During this evening service we recite together the 'Confessions' to help us remember our sins. One is in the form of an alphabetical list. Another, the 'Al Het', is longer and divided into sections. Here is part of it:

> For the sin we have committed before You by hatred
> without cause.
> And for the sin we have committed before You by envy.
> For the sin we have committed before You by betraying
> trust.
> And for the sin we have committed before You by false
> pride.
> For the sin we have committed before You by judging
> others too readily.
> And for all the sins we have committed before You
> unconsciously.
> For all these sins, forgiving God, forgive us, pardon us,
> grant us atonement.

Note how we confess together. There is a feeling that we are not alone in not being perfect and that we can support one another. Note too that we see God as 'forgiving'.

The morning service
The following morning everyone reassembles, already hungry and thirsty, for a full day of prayer. The morning service has many additional prayers and the 'Confessions' are repeated. For

Rosh Hashanah and Yom Kippur

much of the service the doors of the Ark remain open and the congregation remain standing, emphasizing the 'specialness' of the day.

The reading from the Torah is an account of the ritual of the scapegoat (see Leviticus 16:7-10) and of the Day of Atonement as it was observed in ancient times (see Leviticus 23:26-32).

Yizkor

For many Jewish people the part of the service known as 'Yizkor' has a particular importance. It is the time when special prayers are said for parents who have died. Often those whose parents are both still living leave the synagogue for a little while. A special prayer is also said for other relations who have died and, nowadays, a prayer is often said for the six million Jews who were killed during the Nazi holocaust.

The Yom Kippur Musaf service

As at Rosh Hashanah, there is a musaf, or additional, service in remembrance of the additional sacrifice which used to be made at the time when the Temple stood in Jerusalem. This includes the reading of the ancient account in the Talmud (a collection of teachings) of the Yom Kippur sacrifices as they were performed by the High Priest in those days. This description was recorded in the Talmud as precisely as possible so that people should not forget how it was done in case the Temple was rebuilt, as the writers of the Talmud hoped.

In those days the services included the ritual of the scapegoat, described in the Torah reading. In fact the High Priest performed several sacrifices on Yom Kippur, after spending a week in prayer and study to prepare himself. On ten occasions during Yom Kippur the High Priest used to say out loud the sacred name of God and the people would kneel down and say, 'Blessed be His Name, whose glorious kingdom is for ever.' At no other time was the sacred name spoken and it is still never used by Jews.

For nearly two thousand years there has been no Temple, nor a High Priest, nor any sacrifices. But when that special moment is recounted in the story the minister and many members of the congregation will kneel down in remembrance. This is the only time that Jewish people ever kneel when praying.

The blessing by the priests

The very long service finishes with the blessing of all the congregation by the *cohanim* who are descended from the priests who used to take part in the services in the days of the Temple. They are not the same as a Rabbi. They stand in front of the Ark, arms outstretched, and repeat the blessing:

> *The Lord bless you and keep you; the Lord make his face to shine upon you and be gracious unto you; the Lord turn his face unto you and give you peace.*

The afternoon service

After a short break the afternoon service starts with the reading of Chapter 18 of the Book of Leviticus. This seems a strange choice for it deals with forbidden sexual relationships, but it was probably chosen as a reminder of the need for purity in our lives.

This is followed by the reading of the whole Book of Jonah. The story of how Jonah was swallowed by a fish (not a whale, as is often believed) is famous. More important, however, is that Jonah, who is really the people of Israel, was saved and sent by God to warn the people of Nineveh who, because they listened and repented, were also saved by Israel's God. It tells us that not only should we be sorry for our own sins but that we have to be concerned for all the evil that goes on in the world.

Neilah

As the day draws to a close the final service of 'Neilah' starts. Neilah means 'closing' and refers to the closing of the gates of the Temple in ancient times, daily at sunset. Nowadays the closing of the gates is purely symbolic. It is the time when God makes a final decision on our 'account'.

The service, in fact, starts with the doors of the Ark wide open and all the congregation stand as a sign of respect. The prayers remind us that God is kind and forgiving, always ready to 'keep

Delivering flowers in Israel: it is the custom amongst Jews in Israel to send flowers to one another at New Year

Rosh Hashanah and Yom Kippur

the gates open' to those who are willing to change their ways. The confessions are repeated one more time. A last plea is made:

> *In the Book of Life, Blessing, Peace, Prosperity, may we, and all the people of the House of Israel, be remembered and sealed before You, to a happy life and peace.*

Breaking the fast

The end of Yom Kippur, and the end of the fast, is marked by the blowing of the shofar for the last time – a long blast, a soul-stirring reminder of the need to repent and do good in the world.

The fast has to be broken carefully, usually with something like a cup of tea, because by now people are feeling very tired and very hungry. They will also most likely have a headache because they are very thirsty too. On the other hand there is a feeling of exhilaration from the knowledge that you have cleansed yourself in a special and different way. In addition you know that you did it from your own choice and you can actually feel grateful that thirst and hunger were only for one day. It reminds you of others, far less fortunate, for whom hunger and thirst go on day after day.

There is still one thing left to do before collapsing into bed. People make a start on building their succah, the simple hut that will be used in five days' time for the festival of Succot. Already we are looking forward to the next event in the religious cycle.

Rosh Hashanah greetings cards

Rosh Hashanah and Yom Kippur

Succot and Simchat Torah

Lynne Scholefield

Contents

Introduction

Have you ever camped in your own garden? Perhaps you put up a tent or made your own with a clothes-horse and blankets. Did you eat a meal in your shelter with your friends or your brothers and sisters? If you were very lucky you may have been allowed to sleep out there on a warm night.

Every year at Succot, Jewish families celebrate the harvest in this way. Shelters are put up near the house and the family eats, and sometimes sleeps, in them during the festival. At the end of Succot there is another very special day called Simchat Torah. For Jews, this is one of the happiest days of the year.

Succot prayers at the Western Wall

Succot and Simchat Torah

1

The Festival

The Jewish New Year begins in September or October (see page 3). During the first month, called Tishri, there are many important times. The first day of the new year is called Rosh Hashanah, and ten days later comes Yom Kippur. In English this is the Day of Atonement. On Yom Kippur Jews observe a total fast for over twenty-four hours and pray in the synagogue, asking God for forgiveness for any things that they, or anyone else in the community, may have done wrong. Such prayers are not thought to be of much value unless beforehand people have made a real effort to put right any wrongs that exist between them. It is a time for making up quarrels and mending bad relationships.

As soon as Yom Kippur is over it is time to prepare for Succot. Autumn is the time when the last of the year's harvest is collected, and Succot is a harvest festival. It is a time to thank God for providing food, a time for joy and celebration.

As part of the celebrations families put up a shelter – or, more correctly, an extra room – in their gardens. In Hebrew (the Jewish language) the word for a shelter, booth or hut is 'succah'. Succah also means 'tabernacle'. The plural is 'succot' and so the name of the festival simply means 'shelters', 'tabernacles', 'booths' or 'huts'.

The succah has to last for seven days. Sometimes it is quite separate from the house, sometimes it is built on to the house and may even be entered by a door from inside the house.

Bricks and mortar are not used for the succah. They are for

permanent buildings. Wood is a good material, either to build a frame on to which canvas or hardboard can be nailed, or to make the walls (like those of a wooden garage or shed). The roof is never solid. It is made of leafy branches so that at night the stars can be seen. Rarely does it keep out the rain!

Nothing more needs to be done to the outside, but inside, the succah is decorated by all the members of the family. It is very special to live in a room you have made yourself. Fruit and vegetables are hung from the roof and around the walls as a reminder of the harvest. Many other things are also used, such as posters, paper-chains, coloured lights, cards, flags, paintings and drawings.

Very little furniture is needed in the succah – just a table and some chairs. Once everything is ready, the special activities of Succot can take place.

Jewish life is based on Torah. This is the Hebrew word for the Scriptures, which are the first five books of the Bible, called Genesis, Exodus, Leviticus, Numbers and Deuteronomy. These contain all the laws which tell the Jews how God wants them to live, as well as the oldest stories of their traditions.

During the festival blessings are said which remind the Jews of the laws about Succot and also thank God for what He has provided. Because God has given food and shelter it is important not to keep these things to oneself but to share them with others. Visitors are invited to eat with the family in the succah and gifts of food are sometimes taken to the synagogue.

בַּסֻּכֹּת תֵּשְׁבוּ
שִׁבְעַת יָמִים כָּל־הָאֶזְרָח בְּיִשְׂרָאֵל יֵשְׁבוּ בַּסֻּכֹּת: לְמַעַן
יֵדְעוּ דֹרֹתֵיכֶם כִּי בַסֻּכּוֹת הוֹשַׁבְתִּי אֶת־בְּנֵי יִשְׂרָאֵל בְּהוֹצִיאִי
אוֹתָם מֵאֶרֶץ מִצְרָיִם אֲנִי יְהוָה אֱלֹהֵיכֶם:

You shall live in booths (succot) seven days; all citizens in Israel shall live in booths in order that future generations may know that I made the Israelite people live in booths when I brought them out of the land of Egypt. I am the Lord your God.

(Leviticus 23:42–3)

Succot and Simchat Torah

Children in their family succah (shelter)

A modern succah. A perspex dome usually covers the skylight in this flat. At Succot it is removed and replaced with greenery and decorations.

For seven days the family and friends eat in the succah whenever they can. At the beginning of the meal there are blessings. Some of these may be used at any Jewish meal and some are special to Succot.

The mother of the family says a blessing as she lights the candles on the table and the father recites several more. Like all Jewish blessings, they are said in Hebrew and are sometimes chanted to special tunes. Here you can see the blessing related to the law of Leviticus 23:42, first in Hebrew, then with the English letters so that you know roughly how to pronounce it in

Hebrew. In addition there is a traditional tune and a translation into English.

בָּרוּךְ אַתָּה, יְיָ אֱלֹהֵינוּ, מֶלֶךְ הָעוֹלָם, אֲשֶׁר קִדְּשָׁנוּ בְּמִצְוֹתָיו, וְצִוָּנוּ לֵישֵׁב בַּסֻּכָּה:

Ba - rukh a - tah A - do - nai E - lo -
he - nu Me-lekh ha-o - lam____ a-sher kid' - sha - nu be-mitz-vo-
tav ve - tzi - va - nu le - shev ba - suk - kah.___

Blessed are You, Lord our God, King of the Universe, who sanctifies us with His commandments and commands us to sit in the succah.

The kiddush, a blessing that is often used, is recited over the wine, some of which is then drunk by everyone. The two loaves are uncovered and the final blessing, called 'ha-Motzi', is sung. Some of the bread is shared and the proper meal can then begin. After the meal a prayer of thanksgiving is said. In the evening family and friends will stay in the succah talking, telling stories and singing.

The Four Species

There is another law in Leviticus 23 which relates to Succot. This says,

> *On the first day you shall take the fruit of goodly trees, branches of palm trees, boughs of leafy trees and willows of the brook, and you shall rejoice before the Lord your God seven days.*
>
> (Leviticus 23:40)

The family will buy what are known as the 'Four Species' mentioned in this text. The aim is to obtain the most beautiful, elegant and perfect example of each. These are held in the hands and waved as the blessings and psalms are said.

The fruit people buy for this occasion is the etrog, which is a large citrus fruit, very like a lemon in its colour and smell but larger and with a bumpy skin. Etrogs grow mainly in Israel. Choosing and buying the Four Species are the subject of many Jewish stories. In Israel and the United States of America,

The etrog and lulav market, Tel Aviv

where most of the world's Jews live, there will be plenty of choice. In other parts of the world it will be difficult to find even one etrog.

The etrog should have a 'pittam'. This is the brown piece at the base of the stem where the fruit was attached to the plant. The etrog should be a good yellow colour and there should be no blemishes or spots. It is good if the skin is evenly bumpy. Even when the festival is over the etrog can be used. You can make etrog marmalade or wine, or you can stick cloves into the skin, let it dry out and use it for Havdalah (the ceremony at the end of Shabbat).

The palm should be at least 35 cm long with a solid backbone. Both the myrtle and the willow should be at least 24 cm long. The myrtle must have three branches and the willow needs two.

Finally, before the Four Species can be used, the palm, myrtle and willow must be bound together. So that the palm leaves do not spread out they are bound in three places. The

Etrogs for export from Israel being carefully checked

Succot and Simchat Torah

bands are usually made from palm leaves. At the bottom more leaves form the holder for the myrtle and the willow, although these days it is possible to get imitation holders made of plastic!

Now the lulav is ready to use. It is a mitzvah (a commandment) to wave it on each of the first seven days of Succot. Of course, there is a blessing to be said. You may be able to guess what it is by looking at the example on p.28. Nearly all the blessings begin the same way. The ending refers to the action which is about to be performed. This is what you do:

1. Stand facing east.
2. Hold the lulav in front of you (etrog in the left hand; palm, myrtle and willow in the right). By reaching out and back again, shake it three times.
3. Repeat the same movement three times to your right (south), three times behind you over your shoulder (west) and three times to your left (north).
4. Raise the lulav up above you three times and finally lower it down below you three times.

On each day of the festival except Shabbat (the Jewish Sabbath), the lulav and the etrog are waved in all directions to show that God's goodness is everywhere. They are also taken to the synagogue, where they are waved during the chanting of the Hallel psalms (Psalms 113–118; these are recited at every festival). There may also be a succah at the synagogue and some Jewish families will make the Kiddush there rather than in their own succah.

On each of the seven days of Succot special prayers are added to the morning service. These are called Hoshanot. People walk round the inside of the synagogue carrying the lulav and etrog, and saying, 'Save, we beseech You. For Your sake, our God, save, we beseech You.'

On the seventh day, called Hoshana Rabbath, there are seven circuits of the synagogue. People carry willows as well as the lulav, and when they have walked round seven times they beat the leaves of the willows off their stems. This is a sombre moment in a festival of joy and happiness. It is a final ritual which relates back to Yom Kippur and the prayers for forgiveness.

With this the seven days of celebrating in the succah and the waving of the lulav and etrog are completed, but the festival continues for two more days. The ninth day is Simchat Torah. This means 'celebrating (or rejoicing) in the Law'. It is an occasion which developed in medieval times and it brings the whole community, both young and old, together in the synagogue to rejoice in God's Word.

Simchat Torah

In any synagogue the focal point is the Ark, which is a large cupboard containing the Torah scrolls. The Torah scroll, handwritten in Hebrew, is read during the year at the morning services on Mondays, Thursdays and on Shabbat. On Simchat Torah the cycle of readings is completed and a new cycle begins straight away so that it can never be said that there is a time when Jews are not reading Torah. (The Sikh tradition is almost identical. See *Guru Nanak's Birthday* in this series.)

Primary school children visiting a synagogue. The Ten Commandments are written on the stone tablets above the Ark, which contains the Torah scrolls.

Succot and Simchat Torah

People singing and dancing in the Simchat Torah procession, Mount Zion

Jewish days begin at sunset (see *Shabbat* in this series). On Simchat Torah there are at least three services a day. Verses from the Torah are recited aloud by individual members of the congregation and are then repeated by everyone. Then all the Torah scrolls (each containing the whole Torah) are taken out of the Ark and carried round the synagogue in a series of seven processions. These are called ha-Kafot (encircling). The congregation sings and small children carry apples and wave special flags. (See p.101.) The people carrying the scrolls also

Succot and Simchat Torah

sing and sometimes dance with the Torah. It can take a very long time and can be exciting as well as exhausting for some.

Finally all but one of the scrolls are returned to the Ark. From the remaining one the final chapters of the Book of Deuteronomy are read. This is the last section of the Torah and this is the only time in the year that Torah is read aloud in the synagogue at night.

In the morning the seven ha-Kafot are repeated. Afterwards three scrolls are kept out of the Ark. From the first scroll the last portion, Deuteronomy 33–34, will be read again. Many people from the congregation are called to say a blessing, thanking God for giving the Torah. This is an 'aliyah', which literally means 'going up' to where the scroll of the Torah is placed.

The fifth aliyah is given to all the young children, who together come up to the bimah (the platform) where the Torah is read. A large prayer shawl, or tallit, is spread over their heads as they recite the blessing. The last person to be called up has a very special honour. He is the one who completes the cycle of Torah readings for the year. He may be a prominent person in the community or he may be having a celebration (a simha) or there may be some other reason. On this occasion he is called Chatan Torah, 'the Bridegroom of the Torah'.

The second scroll now replaces the first and Genesis 1:1–2:3 is read by a new reader. He is called Chatan Bereshit, 'the Bridegroom of the Beginning'. The new cycle of reading has begun.

The service does not end here. There is a reading from the third scroll. This is Numbers 29:35–30:4. It includes the laws about the final day of the festival of Succot.

When all the scrolls have been put back in the Ark the story of Joshua is read. The Book of Joshua is in the Jewish Bible, but is not part of the Torah. Joshua became the leader of the Jews when Moses died. His story is a reminder that Judaism has continued and developed since the time when the Torah was completed. That happened during the forty years which the Jews spent wandering in the desert after they had been freed from Egypt. The story of those years is told in the next chapter.

Succot and Simchat Torah

2

The Story

'God says to Israel, "My children, reside in the succah for seven days so that you may remember the miracles which I did for you in the desert."'

Deserts are strange places. There are no roads, few plants and little water. During the day the sun beats down and at night it can be icy cold. In the desert much is stripped away. A person who goes into the desert and survives is often changed. Many people discover God there.

The story behind Succot is the story of a whole people who entered the desert as escaped slaves and whose descendants came out after forty years as a strong nation. They encountered God and learned, slowly, to follow His laws and to trust Him.

The story began in Egypt and this is a brief summary of how it is told in the Book of Exodus (Exodus means 'exit' or 'going out'). After many years as slaves of the Egyptians the Israelites, as the Jews were then called, were set free by God through Moses and promised a land of their own. Led by Moses, they began the journey. They were glad to be free but they were frightened of what lay ahead. When they reached the Red Sea the Egyptian army was close behind. Thousands of soldiers and over six hundred chariots were chasing them. It seemed that they were all going to die and it was all Moses' fault.

'We told you,' they said. 'We should have stayed in Egypt. It would have been better to remain slaves in Egypt than to die in the desert.'

Moses had not lost hope. 'Don't be frightened,' he said. 'Stand firm and see the way God will save you today. You will never see the Egyptians again. God will fight for you and you have only to be still.'

And that is what happened. It was the first miracle of the desert. A cloud came between the Egyptians and the Israelites. Moses, directed by God, stretched out his hand over the sea and the waters parted. The Israelites walked through unharmed but the Egyptians, who tried to follow them, were drowned. Now the people were impressed. They forgot what they had said to Moses and joined him in a song of praise.

The Lord is my strength and my song,
And He has become my salvation.
This is my God, and I will praise Him,
My father's God and I will exalt Him.

Moses led them away from the Red Sea. By day they followed a pillar of cloud and at night there was a pillar of fire to give them light. Perhaps they thought their troubles were over. Their excitement and delight in their freedom lasted just three days. Then they complained to Moses again.

'We're thirsty. The water here isn't fresh. What are we going to drink?'

Moses asked God, who told him to throw a particular tree into the water. The water became sweet. God also made it clear that there were certain conditions to this journey. Moses spoke to the people again.

'None of the harm which came to the Egyptians will affect you,' he said, 'if you will listen to the voice of God and follow His laws.' But it was to take a very long time for them to learn to become God's people.

They had been in the desert for six weeks when the next big problem had to be faced. The people were hungry. They brought their complaints to Moses and his brother, Aaron.

Succot and Simchat Torah

'We should have stayed in Egypt. We had plenty to eat there. It's your fault if we starve to death in this desert.'

It was really God they were complaining about. Moses told Aaron to say to the people, 'Come before God with your complaints.'

Suddenly everyone felt how near God was. Moses told them that they would have meat for supper that night, and bread for their breakfast. In the evening a flock of birds, quails, flew into the camp. The Israelites killed them and roasted them on the fires.

When they woke up next morning the ground was covered with a white sticky substance.

'What is it?' everyone asked.

'It is the bread which God has given you,' Moses explained. 'Gather up just enough for today. Don't hoard any.'

They called it 'manna', which means 'What is it?' in Hebrew, or, as we might say in English, 'whatsit'.

When the Israelites ground it up and baked it the manna tasted like biscuits made with honey. Everyone had plenty to eat but some people tried to store it up for the following day. It went mouldy and was full of maggots.

Moses was angry. Fresh manna was lying on the ground waiting to be collected but some people preferred to do things their own way rather than to trust God.

There was one other instruction about the manna. The seventh day, or Shabbat, was a day of rest when no one should work. During Friday everybody was to gather enough manna for two days. It would not go rotten. On Shabbat everyone would rest as God Himself had rested when He created the world. (See *Shabbat* in this series.)

The people continued their journey towards Sinai but it was three months before they stood at the foot of the sacred mountain. Here they were to receive God's laws.

God had already revealed Himself as one who brings freedom to the oppressed and as an enemy of injustice. Now, according to the Book of Exodus they would know Him as a God who is 'full of compassion and pity, who is not easily angered and who shows great love and faithfulness' (Exodus 34:6).

The people were told to prepare themselves very carefully and to wait at the bottom of the mountain. There was thunder and lightning, the sound of a trumpet and dark smoke. God said, 'I am the Lord God who brought you out of Egypt where you were slaves. Worship no god but Me.' Then came the other great commandments:

Do not make images to worship.
Do not use My name for evil purposes.
Remember the Sabbath day and keep it holy.
Respect your father and your mother.
Do not murder.
Do not commit adultery.
Do not steal.
Do not accuse anyone falsely.
Do not crave after anything which belongs to someone else.
(Exodus 20:1–17; Deuteronomy 5:1–21)

The people were terrified. 'Do not let God speak to us or we will die,' they said to Moses. 'You speak to us. We will listen.'

So Moses went up into the darkness of the cloud at the top of Mount Sinai and God gave him the other laws. There were instructions about worship, the rights of slaves, manslaughter and injury to human life, theft and damage to property, social and religious duties, justice and human rights.

Right at the end came details about the three great festivals: Pesach (or Passover), Shavuot and Succot. God said that if the people followed all the laws He would give them the Promised Land and make them a great nation.

Moses explained this to the Israelites and they promised they would keep every law. This agreement is called the Covenant.

God now spoke to Moses about the tabernacle and the Ark. The tabernacle, a large tent, was to be the Israelites' place of

Mount Sinai

worship. They were to set it up wherever they stopped to rest. Inside the tabernacle they were to place the Ark of the Covenant, a box made of acacia wood and decorated with gold.

When God had finished speaking to Moses on Mount Sinai He gave him two stone tablets on which were engraved His commandments. These were to be kept in the Ark of the Covenant.

Because Moses was away for so long the people became restless. They broke one of the laws they had promised to keep. They melted down their jewellery and made a golden calf to worship.

Moses came down the mountainside carrying the tablets of stone. When he got near to the camp he heard the singing and dancing. Then he saw the idol the people were worshipping. He threw down the tablets and they shattered into pieces. Then he destroyed the calf. He ground it to dust and scattered it in the water the people had to drink.

Moses went to the top of Mount Sinai to beg forgiveness for his people. There he received a second set of stone tablets. When he finally returned the people were afraid to go near him because his face shone with a strange light.

Succot and Simchat Torah 39

Now at last they set off northwards towards the land of Canaan. But soon there were more complaints about the food and again many of the people began to look back to the time of slavery in Egypt and to recall it in a very rosy light. They were still complaining when they reached the borders of the Promised Land and this was to have serious results.

Moses sent men to spy out the land and to bring back reports.

'It is a land flowing with milk and honey,' they said, showing him the fruit they had brought back. 'Yet the people who live there are very strong. The cities are large and well fortified. We cannot fight against them; they are too powerful.'

Once more everyone turned to Moses. 'It is hopeless,' they said. 'We are all going to die. It is all Moses' fault.' Finally, unable to trust Moses or God, they said, 'Let's choose another leader and go back to Egypt.'

The Covenant had been broken and finally God's anger was shown. The people still needed to be taught to trust God. They were to go back into the desert and travel there for forty years. No one who had despised God's promise that day could ever enter the land flowing with milk and honey. Their descendants might inherit the land but they could not, not even Moses, for even he had at times doubted God's word. He could lead them to the very borders of the land God had promised them. He would be able to see the land but he would never enter it.

And so it was that after forty years of wandering in the desert the Jews, as they were later to be called, were ready to enter the Promised Land. Those forty years had been years of great difficulty. It was the children and the grandchildren of the original slaves who were to inherit the land of Israel. It was Joshua and not Moses who was to lead them to triumph. Always they would remember those who had suffered in the wanderings and who, in their life in the desert, had learned so much about God.

This is why, to this day, Jews celebrate the festival of Succot, and why at Simchat Torah they rejoice at the reading of God's laws and their tradition and finish with the story of Joshua.

Succot and Simchat Torah

3

Meanings

Meanings of the Four Species

The Four Species have been used at Succot for more than three thousand years. Many different meanings have been given to them. The four together are said to represent the four-letter name of God. This is so holy that it is never pronounced.

Each of the species is also an allusion to God, and is linked with a verse in the Bible referring to God:

Etrog – because it is written in Psalm 104:1 'You are clothed in glory and majesty.'

Palm – because it is written in Psalm 92:12: 'The righteous bloom like a palm tree.'

Myrtle – because it is written in Zechariah 1:8: 'And he stood among myrtle trees.'

Willow – because it is written in Psalm 68:4: 'Praise Him who rides on the clouds [avarot], the Lord is His name.'

The rabbis also saw meanings connected with parts of the body, each of which can be used to serve God:

Etrog – heart – *place of understanding and wisdom*

Palm – spine – *uprightness*

Myrtle – eyes – *enlightenment*

Willow – mouth – *prayer*

In yet another interpretation the Four Species are said to symbolize the four elements:

Etrog, which is yellow, resembles *fire.*

Palm, which grows straight into the sky, means *air.*

Myrtle, which grows close to the ground, symbolizes *earth.*

Willow, which grows beside rivers, represents *water.*

Finally, they are sometimes said to symbolize different types of people. Taste represents learning. Smell represents good deeds. The etrog has both taste and smell, like those who have learning and do good deeds. The palm has taste and no smell, symbolizing those who have learning but no good deeds. The myrtle has only fragrance, like those who do good deeds but have no learning. The willow has neither taste nor smell, and in the same way there are some

Etrog and lulav

people who lack both learning and good deeds. When the Four Species are bound together it is like a community of different types of people united with one another. A thirteenth-century collection of sayings includes these words:

Just as a man cannot fulfil his duty at Succot unless all Four Species are bound together, so Israel cannot be redeemed until all Jews hold together.

You should be now be wondering why the ritual of the Four Species is performed. The Jewish religion encourages people to ask 'Why?' or 'What does it mean?' We have already seen that there are many different answers about the meaning of the Four Species. There are also several different reasons why the lulav is waved.

The first is very simple. Waving the lulav is an expression of joy and thanksgiving at harvest time. People often wave their arms when they are pleased or excited. Secondly, because the lulav is waved in every direction it is a symbol that God is everywhere, that it is God's world and His harvest.

SUCCOT SONG
ILO ORLEANS

It's harvest time,
It's harvest time,
How rich is nature's yield
In fruit of earth
and bush and tree,
From orchard, farm and field.

It's autumn time,
It's autumn time,
When leaves turn gold and red.
In smiling sky
And land and sea
God's glories are outspread.

It's Succot time,
It's Succot time,
This day of our thanksgiving.
We hymn the praise
Of God above
For all the joys of living.

Finally, the lulav is waved because God has commanded it. It is waved slowly and with concentration. Body, mind and will combine to praise God, Who is all around. As the lulav is drawn inwards it is as though God's peace and presence are also being drawn into us from every direction. At one point during the service, as the lulav is being waved, these words are said: 'Give thanks to the Lord for He is God, for His loving-kindness endures for ever.'

Meanings of the festival

The festival of Succot itself has several meanings. Living in the succah is a reminder of the time in history when the Jews (then known as Israelites) made their journey through the desert. They lived in tents and learned to rely on God. They themselves never entered the Promised Land, but because of their trials and tribulations later generations experienced freedom and greater happiness.

Succot is also a harvest festival, a time to thank God for what He has provided and to pray for good crops in the coming year. The fruit and vegetables which decorate the succah link the two and help those who see them to be conscious of the beauty of the world.

Succot is one of the three great pilgrimage festivals in Judaism. The other two are Pesach (Passover) and Shavuot (the Feast of Weeks). The Torah says,

Three times in the year you shall keep a feast to me... three times in the year shall all your males appear before the Lord God.
(Exodus 23:14, 17)

For many hundreds of years Jews made the pilgrimage to the Temple in Jerusalem to keep this commandment. At times Succot was the most popular of the three festivals. Three thousand years ago Solomon chose Succot as the festival at which to dedicate the first Temple in Jerusalem. But five hundred years later the festival had fallen into disuse and we find Ezra trying to restore it. Another five hundred years after that the Jewish historian Josephus was calling Succot 'the holiest and greatest of the Hebrew feasts'.

Succot and Simchat Torah

In the year 70 C.E. (C.E. means 'Common Era') the Romans destroyed Jerusalem and much of its Temple. Those Jews who were still alive after five years of bitter fighting were sent into exile. The Dispersion (Diaspora) of the Jews had begun and sixty years later, in 130 C.E., the Romans made it an offence for any Jew to live in Palestine. The Temple, once the focus of all worship, was totally destroyed. But Judaism did not die. The rabbis began to collect together all their teaching and the interpretations of Torah – the Law and the tradition. These were written down and are called the Talmud. In the Talmud we can find many references to Succot and there is a whole section which deals with what the Talmud calls 'THE festival'.

Perhaps Succot remains such a popular festival because it is a time of joy. The Torah calls it 'the season of our rejoicing'. The decoration of the succah, the food and the rituals add to the celebration of the harvest. But the joy is tempered by the awareness that it is autumn and that winter is approaching. Winter has always been a symbol of death. The days get shorter. It is cold and nothing grows. The ritual of Succot includes the prayer for the dead (yizkor), and on the eighth day, Shemeni Atseret, there is a prayer for rain:

May He send rain from the heavenly source to soften the earth with its crystal drops. . . . For You are the Lord our God who caused the wind to blow and the rain to fall. For a blessing and not a curse. For life and not for death. For plenty and not for scarcity.

But at Simchat Torah, the last day of the festival, rejoicing returns in full. It is rejoicing in Torah (law and tradition) itself and for having lived through another year, another cycle of that tradition.

Now there is a new year ahead. It brings hope but it also brings fear and uncertainty. On Shabbat during Succot the Book of Ecclesiastes is read. This book of wisdom reminds us how short and uncertain life can be. The festival reflects the whole of life in miniature.

For everything there is a season and a time for every purpose
  under heaven:
A time to be born, and a time to die;
A time to plant, and a time to reap;
A time to kill, and a time to heal;
A time to break down, and a time to build up;
A time to weep, and a time to laugh;
A time to mourn, and a time to dance;
A time to cast away stones, and a time to gather stones together;
A time to embrace, and a time to refrain from embracing;
A time to seek, and a time to lose;
A time to keep, and a time to cast away;
A time to rend, and a time to sew;
A time to keep silence, and a time to speak;
A time to love, and a time to hate;
A time for war, and a time for peace.

(Ecclesiastes 3:1–8)

Carrying the scrolls round the synagogue at Simchat Torah

Succot and Simchat Torah

On each day the Hoshanot are said: 'Save, we beseech You. For Your sake, our God, save, we beseech You.' These prayers are recited while people walk round the synagogue. It is the custom to wear the tallit (prayer shawl) over one's head. The circuits of the synagogue are a reminder of the processions around the altar in the Temple in Jerusalem. The past is brought into the present. On a personal level this ceremony can be very powerful and unsettling. The rhythm of the ritual and the expressiveness of the prayer can immerse one in a sense of timelessness and contact with God.

This is the festival which also points to the future, not just for Jews but for everyone. Succot comes at the end of the agricultural year and symbolizes the end of time as we know it. It also symbolizes the time of peace (shalom) which will follow. Just as the fruits of the harvest are gathered into the succah, so God will gather all the nations under His Succah of Peace. In the days of the Temple, when there were sacrifices, seventy bullocks were offered during Succot. These represented the seventy known nations of the world. The Book of Zechariah, which is read on the first day of Succot, says:

And the Lord will become King over all the earth; on that day the Lord will be One and His name one.

(Zechariah 14:9)

Then everyone that survives of all the nations that have come against Jerusalem shall go up year after year to worship the King, the Lord of hosts, and to keep the feast of Succot.

(Zechariah 14:16)

An essential part of the festival is hospitality. People invite guests to join them for a meal in the succah. Some Jews also follow a custom called 'ushpizin', a symbolic invitation. Each night a different Biblical figure is asked to visit the succah. These are Abraham, Isaac, Jacob, Joseph, Moses, Aaron and David. Special posters which can be used to decorate the succah show the words of this ritual invitation.

Many of these ideas are combined in the meaning of the succah. The design of the roof uses branches. This allows the stars to shine through as a reminder that all blessings come from heaven. The whole building should shake in the wind to remind people of the time when they were in the desert, living in huts and wholly dependent on God. It is also a reminder that life does not last forever. Even if we spend our lives in one place we are still on a journey, a pilgrimage. By the end of the festival the succah should have been used to the full. Each day a guest has been invited and the peace of the succah shared with all. The succah is then stored away in the hope that it will not be needed again. If the Messiah comes all will sit under the Succah of Shalom.

Succot is no longer the most popular festival in some countries. But in others it is still very important. In the former Soviet Union, for example, there were often demonstrations on Simchat Torah. Russian Jews remembered that they were first and foremost Jews and looked to their fellow Jews in other countries to support them. Like Jews everywhere, they still regarded 'Eretz Israel', the Land of Israel, as the Promised Land, and because they were not allowed to visit it, they saw themselves as 'still wandering in the desert'. At Succot especially they looked forward to the time when their Dispersion would be over and they too would be free to return 'home' if they so wished.

Succot and Simchat Torah

Chanukah

Lynne Scholefield

Contents

Introduction

When was the last time you saw a candle? Perhaps it was on a cake, or decorating a table for a special meal. If you think back there are certain to be events and times which stand out in your mind. How are important events celebrated in your family? Do you have candles on your birthday cake to show how old you are, or fireworks in the autumn, or fairy lights on a tree in winter?

In every Jewish family there is a celebration with lights each year. It helps them remember important things which happened to Jews in Israel a long time ago. The festival is called Chanukah (with the Ch pronounced as in lo*ch*), a Hebrew word. There is a story to be told, special food to eat, presents, games *and* candles.

The first night of Chanukah

Chanukah

1

A Typical Chanukah

It is December and in the northern hemisphere the days are short. The weather is cold but often it is bright and clear. As the sun sets, lights come on and curtains are drawn. But not in Jewish houses. There, as the light fades, the family gathers in the living-room. In the window there is a candlestick. It has nine holders, each at the top of a curving branch. Eight of them are level. The ninth one, in the middle, stands apart from the others. On this first night of Chanukah there is a candle in the middle holder and another on the extreme right of the line of eight.

Chanukah is a Jewish festival and, though the things to be used are very ordinary, like candles, they become special when they are linked with the laws which Jews observe. Together, they make up the religion we call Judaism. Chanukah celebrates one particular occasion in the past when the Jews were saved from destruction. Each family can think of other times too, some very recent, when they again needed help.

At the start of the festival there are blessings to be said. As the father of the family begins to recite them everyone in the house feels a sense of belonging to one enormous family with Jews all over the world. They know that these same words are being spoken in thousands, if not millions, of other homes in many countries. Even the language used is the same. The words are spoken in the ancient language of Hebrew. Because of this, the Jewish family feel united, not only with every other

Jewish family in the world today, but with every Jewish family which has celebrated the festival of Chanukah over the past two thousand years. Translated into English, this is what the father says:

Blessed are you, Lord our God, King of the Universe, who has sanctified* us with his commandments and commanded us to kindle the light of Chanukah.

Then he thanks God for the miracles performed in the past at this time of Chanukah. Finally, because this is the first night of the festival, he adds another blessing. It is called the *Shehechiyanu*.

Blessed are you, Lord our God, King of the Universe, who has kept us alive, and preserved us, and enabled us to reach this season.

Now the father lights the middle candle. It is called the 'shamash', or servant candle. Then, when the flame is steady, he uses this to light the first candle in the row of eight and says another short prayer. This candle will burn for at least thirty minutes, its light shining out from the window, clearly visible to anyone passing by.

The festival lasts for eight days. On each night one more candle will be lit so that by the last night all eight will be burning together. The candles are always put in the candlestick from right to left but they are always lit from left to right, the newest candle being lit first from the shamash.

There are many different kinds of Chanukah candlesticks made from wood or metal but almost always eight candles are at the same height to show that all eight days of the festival are of the same importance. The candlestick is known as the 'Chanukah menorah', or more commonly a 'Chanukiyah' (plural: 'Chanukiyot').

*sanctified means 'made holy'.

Chanukah

Presents, songs and dreidels

While the candle burns in the window there are other things going on in the house. At Chanukah it has been a custom for a long time to give money to children. This is called Chanukah 'gelt', or spending money. Nowadays other presents and cards are given as well. And because the festival lasts for eight days and every day is of equal value, a present is given each night to the children. Not surprisingly, they really enjoy this festival!

As the candle burns on this first night of Chanukah the family sings special festival songs. The best known is *Ma'oz Tzur*, written in the thirteenth century and sung to a traditional German tune.

MA'OZ TZUR

Rock of A-ges, let our song Praise Thy sav - ing pow - er;

Thou, a-midst the rag-ing foes, Wast our shelt-'ring tow - er.

Fu-rious, they as - sailed us, But Thine arm a - vailed ___ us,

And Thy word Broke their sword When our own strength failed us.

Other songs follow. They are mostly about games that are played during Chanukah. The most popular games are those played with a 'dreidel', or spinning-top, called in Hebrew a 'svivon'. These can be bought or made. The dreidel has four sides. On each side a Hebrew letter is drawn. After the dreidel has spun, it falls with one side uppermost, like dice. Coins, counters or nuts are put into a central bank. Each player takes it in turn to spin the dreidel.

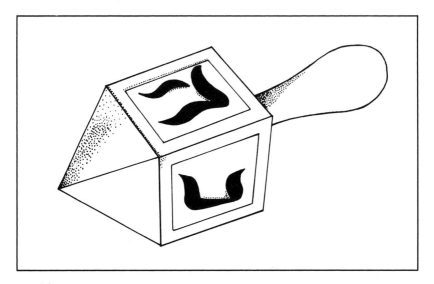

Dreidel

If the letter Nun ‏נ‎ comes up this means 'Take nothing'.
If the letter Gimmel ‏ג‎ comes up this means 'Take all'.
If the letter Heh ‏ה‎ comes up this means 'Take half'.
If the letter Shin ‏שׁ‎ comes up this means 'Put one in'.

This simple gambling game goes on, with players adding to the central bank when it holds only one or no objects, until the winner eventually takes all the coins or tokens.

There are other games that can be played with the dreidel. The Hebrew letters also stand for numbers: Nun=50; Gimmel=3; Heh=5; Shin=300. The players agree a certain target, say 1000, and the first to reach the target exactly is the winner. Some children just play with the dreidel and see who can make it spin the longest.

Chanukah food

Singing, playing games, laughing and talking all work up an appetite. Like nearly all festivals Chanukah has special foods. Traditionally these are associated with oil and dairy produce. In particular at Chanukah time Jewish families like to eat special potato pancakes called 'latkes' or, in Hebrew, 'levitot'. These are fried and eaten hot. A recipe appears at the end of this book (p. 104.)

Latkes

The date of Chanukah

All these things happen on the first night of Chanukah. For families living in Israel there will also be torchlight processions. Large Chanukiyot will be placed on public buildings and lit from torches which have been carried by runners from town to town.

The first night of Chanukah is the twenty-fifth of the Jewish month Kislev. This is nearly always in December. The Jewish year usually begins in September and Kislev is the third month. The festival ends on the second day of Tebet, the fourth month in the Jewish calendar.

Wherever Jews live candles will be lit each night in every home. They are also lit in the synagogue – the Jewish place of worship. Here there will be a special Chanukiyah. During the Shabbat (Sabbath) service which comes at some time during the eight days of Chanukah there are readings from the Torah and from the Book of Numbers. Special prayers and blessings are said. The festival of Chanukah is based on a story which is often told in songs or perhaps as a play performed by children. That story makes up our next chapter.

Young children at a Chanukah party. They are holding dreidels

Chanukah

2

The Chanukah Story

The four letters which are used for the four faces of the dreidel are chosen for a reason. They are the first letters of four Hebrew words which, translated into English, mean: 'A great miracle happened there.'

Nun	‏נ‏	miracle	‏נֵס‏
Gimmel	‏ג‏	a great	‏גָדוֹל‏
Heh	‏ה‏	happened	‏הָיָה‏
Shin	‏שׁ‏	there	‏שָׁם‏

Note: Hebrew is written from right to left so that the first letter of every word is on the right-hand side.

The story of Chanukah tells of that miracle and all that led up to it. But to understand the story we have to travel back in time and imagine the life of Jews in the land of Judah during the second century B.C.E. (Before the Common Era).

In Jerusalem, the capital city, the worship of God was centred on the Temple. Here sacrifices were made and services held. Jews also worshipped in synagogues and in their own homes. People tried to follow the teaching of the Torah – the first five books of what Christians call the Old Testament.

The Torah lays out in detail how people should show their love for the one and only God by keeping His laws and traditions. To follow these ways is what it means to be a Jew. Some laws are outstandingly important. For example, Shabbat (the Sabbath) – from sunset on Friday to Saturday night – has always been kept as a special day, different from the rest of the week (see the book on *Shabbat* in this series).

Food laws are also very important. Food is prepared according to certain rules and some foods are totally forbidden. These include pork and bacon, the meat of the pig.

A third custom, observed by Jews as a sign that they are a separate people, is circumcision of all male children when they are eight days old. Circumcision means 'cutting around' and refers to the removal of the foreskin on the penis.

Antiochus Epiphanes

The story of events leading up to Chanukah began in the year 175 B.C.E. The Greeks had ruled over the Jews for a long time but in that year a general named Antiochus became ruler of the Syrian part of the Greek Empire, including Judah. Until now the people of this region had been left alone as long as they paid their taxes and caused no trouble. Many Jews started to follow Greek customs and learned to speak Greek. They used Greek names and played Greek sports but, unlike many other countries in the Greek Empire, they ignored Greek religion because the Torah forbade the worship of other gods. They kept their own religious laws and practices.

Antiochus had a nickname, Epiphanes, meaning 'the shining one' – but the Jews called him Epimanes, 'the mad man'. Perhaps he was mad, though others before and since have attempted to destroy the Jews. It seems that Antiochus believed he was the god Zeus and that everyone in the Empire should worship him. He ordered that all the people must bow down before his statue. But the Jewish law said:

I am the Lord thy God which have brought thee out of the land
of Egypt, out of the house of bondage.
Thou shalt have no other gods before me.
Thou shalt not make unto thee any graven image, or any
likeness of any thing that is in heaven above, or that is in the
earth beneath, or that is in the water under the earth:
Thou shalt not bow down thyself to them, nor serve them: for
I the Lord thy God am a jealous God . . .

Exodus 20:2–5

Some Jews obeyed the order of Antiochus but, despite threats, others refused. Among them was an old priest, Eleazar, who was ninety years old. He was put to death because he would not even pretend to obey the orders; neither would he eat the pork which had been sacrificed in front of the statue. Nor would the seven sons of Hannah, ordinary people but heroes in the story.

The story of Hannah and her sons

Hannah, a widow, had seven sons. Much as she loved them and depended on them she encouraged them one by one to defy the command of Antiochus and to follow the Jewish laws. Each died a horrible death until only Hannah's youngest son was left alive. Antiochus, realizing that his persecution was not being very successful, begged the boy to obey, promising him money and an important job in the government if he did. The boy paid no attention to him. Antiochus then appealed to Hannah to speak to her son. What she said was not quite what Antiochus had in mind. 'Don't be afraid of this butcher,' she called out in front of the crowd. 'Accept death and prove yourself worthy of your brothers.'

The young man died and so did Hannah but their example inspired many others in Israel. Then came a report that Antiochus had been killed in battle in Egypt. The people came out on to the streets in a mood of rebellion and they pulled down all the statues. The report was false. Antiochus returned in 168 B.C.E. and, when he discovered what had happened, gave orders intending to destroy Judaism completely.

First, the Jews were forbidden to study the Torah. Secondly, they were forbidden to circumcise boy babies. They were also forbidden to observe the Shabbat, and finally Antiochus ordered that sacrifices of live pigs had to be made to Zeus.

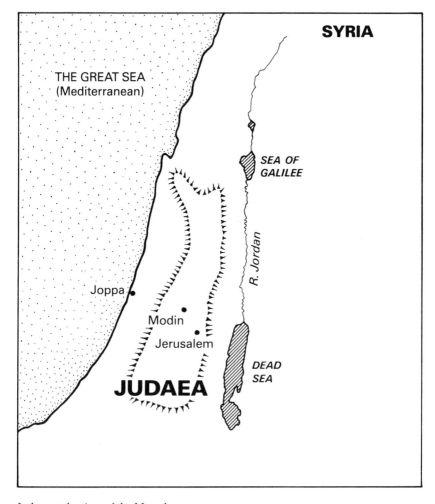

Judaea at the time of the Maccabees

Chanukah

The story of Mattathias

In the hills of Judaea, north-west of Jerusalem, there is a small town called Modin. Not long after the new orders were given soldiers arrived in the town to see that the pig sacrifice was carried out. People gathered to see what would happen as an elderly priest called Mattathias was told to begin the sacrifice. He was a leader in the town and could set an example. The officer in charge offered him rich rewards for carrying out the sacrifice. It was a bad day for that officer. In clear, ringing tones Mattathias declared that he and his family would continue to follow the teachings of the Torah. They were not going to obey the King's instructions.

But if Mattathias would not make the sacrifice there were others who would. Another Jew stepped up to the altar to carry out the officer's command. Mattathias drew a knife, rushed up and killed him as a traitor to Israel and Judaism. Then he turned and knifed the officer. The crowd dealt with the soldiers. Rebellion had begun. Mattathias and his sons pulled down the altar and fled into the hills of the Judaean wilderness.

Back in Jerusalem, Antiochus set up his statues and altars in the Temple and made pig sacrifices there – the holiest place of the Jews. He took little notice of what had happened in the little town of Modin but more and more men were leaving their families to join Mattathias in the hills. The rebellion was growing, gaining strength all the time.

It was a hard life moving from place to place in the wilderness. Mattathias was an old man. It was not long before he became ill and died. His son Judas took over. The family were known as the Hasmoneans but Judas was soon given a nickname. He was called Maccabeus, which means 'The Hammerer', and his followers and later his family became known as the Maccabees.

The capture of Jerusalem

Led by Judas, the Maccabees became freedom fighters. At first they fought small 'hit and run' battles, coming down from the hills at night, attacking Syrian camps silently and quickly and running back to the hills before reinforcements could arrive. Or they ambushed Syrian troops sent to look for them in the hills. They were small in number but they knew the land much better than their enemies. Their support grew. More and more men joined them. Soon they began to face the enemy in full-scale battles and gained one victory after another. Gradually they moved nearer and nearer to Jerusalem. Antiochus decided to destroy them once and for all. He collected all his troops together and sent out a vast Syrian army against the Maccabees. The Jews were heavily outnumbered but they were fighting for their own land, for their religious freedom and their independence. The Maccabees took on the might of Antiochus and they won. Jerusalem was free. It seemed like a miracle.

Judas Maccabeus led the victorious Jews into Jerusalem and they began the task of cleansing the Temple. They had to remove all the statues, all the filth of the pig sacrifices and make the holy place pure again. Then they could rededicate their own Jewish altar. The lamp, a symbol of the presence of God who had given them the strength to win the victory, would burn once more. And it must burn for ever. The light must not go out. If it did it would signify that their freedom was short-lived. But there was a problem. It took time to make the specially prepared oil and there was enough for only one day. They lit the lamp regardless and then – A Great Miracle Happened There ‏נ ג ה ש‎ – the oil burned for eight days, by which time more was ready. Their victory was real.

Judas Maccabeus decreed that each year there should be a festival for eight days, beginning on the twenty-fifth day of Kislev, to celebrate the new altar and the new Jewish kingdom. That festival, still celebrated today, is Chanukah, which means 'dedication'.

3

Symbols of Chanukah

Lights shine out in the darkness: one more each night until the whole row is ablaze. The lights are not used to see by but to look at, because Chanukah is a festival of light. The lights in the Chanukiyah are symbols of a victory of good over evil. They stand for freedom and joy and, especially, for life.

Light and dark can mean many things. Think of a dark tunnel, seemingly endless, and then a tiny spot of light which grows and grows. Imagine a time before electric light. As winter comes the hours of daylight get shorter and shorter. It is very cold, and everywhere around you things are dying – the leaves on the trees, plants; some animals no longer have enough to eat. Things are dark, but there is always hope that light and life will return. In the middle of winter in many lands lights blaze out as a symbol of the belief that the darkness will end, and there will be new life.

At Chanukah the lights celebrate the new life which the Jews won, with God's help, for their country. It was a victory of the few over many, of the weak over the strong. It was justice defeating wickedness and the beginning of a new Jewish community. After the first candle has been lit a special prayer is said, called the *Hanerot Hallalu*, which means 'these lights'.

A rabbi lights the Chanukiyah

We light these candles on account of the miracles, the deliverances, and the wonders which you did perform for our fathers through your holy priests. During the whole eight days of Chanukah these candles are sacred and we are not permitted to make any profane use of them, but only to look at them, in order that we may give thanks unto your name, for your miracles, your deliverances and your wonders.

There *is* something special about light. One tiny candle can be seen across a vast distance of darkness, and all the darkness in the world cannot put it out. To light a candle is to make a difference. If the first Chanukah had never happened a great deal would be different. There would be no Jewish faith, or people, and so the two other great religions which developed from Judaism might not exist – there would be no Christianity or Islam.

Chanukah

Other things would have died, too, along with the Shabbat, and the Jewish law. All Jewish beliefs centre on a single idea – that there is one God, creator of the world we live in, and that it is possible for man to know and love Him. This idea has a special name. It is called 'monotheism'. Every Jewish child learns his first Hebrew, and his first religious idea, by saying the Shema. These verses from the sixth chapter of Deuteronomy in the Torah say:

Hear, O Israel, the Lord our God, the Lord is ONE and you shall love the Lord your God with all your heart, and all your soul and all your strength.

Without the lives of Hannah and her sons, and Mattathias and Judas Maccabeus, all that would have been lost – but it was not. Each year the light streams out as a way of saying 'thank you' and as a way for Jews to rededicate themselves to God, to theTorah, and to the future. In the Temple in 165 B.C.E. the lights were rededicated and the festival of Chanukah began.

חֲנֻכָּה = *Chanukah* = *Dedication*

Yet the Chanukah tradition is more than just a story from history. Many times since, the Jewish people have faced the threat of death. The song *Ma'oz Tzur* recalls these times: verse two tells of the slavery in Egypt and the escape led by Moses. The next verse refers to Babylon and the Exile, while verse four tells of Esther and the salvation of the Jews from Haman.

The Jews have faced persecution in many forms: the Romans, the Christians in Spain and Eastern Europe, and more recently during the Holocaust in Hitler's Europe when millions of Jews were killed in concentration camps. But, throughout, the Chanukah tradition has remained as a symbol of the victory of light over darkness, life over death.

Jewish persecution in Hitler's Germany began with scenes like this. A soldier holds a notice: 'Germans, stand up for yourselves – don't buy from Jews!'

Even today, Jews living in some countries feel that their beliefs are threatened – their miracle has not yet come.

4

Chanukah Traditions

Every year for centuries Jews have celebrated Chanukah. It is not surprising that many different customs have arisen in those countries where Jews have settled, or that certain events should have been given several meanings. The rabbis, or Jewish teachers, have long argued over these meanings and have given guidance on the origin of traditions.

The festival lasts for eight days because of the miracle of the lamp, but some rabbis believe that the real miracle was the victory of the small, dedicated Jewish force over the Syrian armies. This fight for religious freedom is symbolized by the way the Chanukiyah is placed in the window each evening. Its light can be seen by those outside; it shines out freely. But there have been many times when Jews have not enjoyed religious freedom. The rabbis told the people that, rather than face punishment, even death, for being Jewish, they should not display the Chanukiyah, for God's law should bring life not death.

The eight lights are placed in a row at the same height because each of the days is equally important. The ninth – the shamash, or servant candle, used to light the others – has another purpose also. The lights are to be enjoyed, to be looked at as a celebration but not to be used for ordinary activities. The rabbis taught that if, by accident, a person used the lights of the Chanukah menorah, then it was the light of the shamash and not the special lights being used.

The last night of Chanukah

During the eight days there will always be at least one Shabbat, or Sabbath. This is the Jewish day of rest and worship and takes place from Friday sunset to Saturday night. During this time no work is done and the Chanukah candles are left unlit. In fact Shabbat begins and ends with the use of special candles, quite different from the Chanukah ones. On Friday night the Chanukiyah is lit, with the appropriate blessings. Then the mother lights two Shabbat candles. On Saturday night the Havdalah candle, with its plaited strands, is lit and the flame is put out with wine to mark the end of the Shabbat. Only then can the Chanukiyah be lit again.

Many of the customs of the festival do not date from the beginning of the celebrations. They date from the Middle Ages, and come from Germany and other Eastern European countries where most Jews lived. The Jews of Europe had their own language called Yiddish, and many Chanukah things have Yiddish names. One example of this is 'gelt' – the money given to children. Originally, it seems children took money to their teachers, or the money was used to pay for poor children to have some schooling.

The 'dreidel', described in Chapter 1, is also a Yiddish word. This spinning-top, called a 'svivon' in Hebrew, was used by Jews at Chanukah in the Middle Ages, though perhaps not in quite the same way as today. In some countries the study of the Torah was forbidden and the dreidel was kept in case soldiers or police called. Instead of discovering the forbidden activity all they found was everyone engaged in a gambling game. Eventually the gambling game was so popular that some rabbis became very concerned. One rabbi said, however, that for people to gamble late into the night was a good thing because it taught people to stay up late and one day they might stay up, not to gamble, but to study the Torah.

To study the Torah is the most important thing in Judaism because of the laws on which the religion is based. They cover every aspect of life including things like food. There are laws of 'kashrut', setting out which animals can or cannot be used as food and the ways they must be slaughtered and prepared. Only animals with cloven hooves and which chew the cud can be eaten. This rules out many animals, particularly the pig. This is the reason why the pig sacrifice which Antiochus Epiphanes tried to force upon the Jews was especially horrible for them.

One of the most important rules in the Torah concerns Shabbat. The commandment says that the Shabbat must be kept holy, or set apart, for God. On that day there is to be no work. The Torah and later Jewish thinkers have set out what is meant by work. Antiochus Epiphanes tried to forbid the keeping of the Shabbat but later, when the rebellion broke out, his army took advantage of it. A group of Jews, called Chassidim, not with Mattathias or his sons, were encamped in the hills of Judah, not far from Jerusalem. They were attacked and killed because they refused to break the Shabbat and fight. When news of this massacre reached Mattathias and Judas they decided that they were struggling for the existence of Judaism and they would not let the Syrians use the Jewish laws to destroy them.

It became clear that the laws in the Torah had to be discussed and considered so each generation knew how they should be applied. The findings were eventually collected in a book called the Talmud. It is in the Talmud that the details of Chanukah and its celebrations are worked out. There is no mention of these in the Torah simply because the Torah was established long before the time of the Maccabean revolt. The story of the revolt is told in the two books of the Maccabees. These form part of a collection of fourteen books called the Apocrypha. They are not normally included as a part of the Old Testament in modern Bibles. Most of the details of the military victory can be found in 1 and 2 Maccabees, but there is no mention of the miracle of the oil lamp burning for eight days. That story is in the Talmud.

It is probable that Chanukah began, in some ways, as an extension of another festival, Tabernacles, which takes place earlier in the year. The synagogue reading from Numbers 7 is about the setting up of the Tabernacle in the wilderness. At one time Chanukah booths were set up, and plants used at the earlier festival were included at Chanukah. The nine-branched Chanukah menorah was no doubt based on the seven-branched menorah which stood in the Temple. It is still a symbol of Israel today.

Other practices are found only in particular countries. For example, in Eastern Europe effigies or dolls representing Antiochus were carried around by children asking for money. At the end of the day the dolls were burnt. In Israel the first torch is lit in the town of Modin and carried by runners to key places throughout the country. Also in Israel, doughnuts, bought hot, are becoming traditional Chanukah food. In Britain and America, where Christmas is such a popular Christian festival, the two celebrations are often compared. They fall so close together in time and share many common features. They are both festivals of light, with present-giving and parties. Both last for a period of several days, and both begin on the evening before the festival day proper. In fact John 10:22 mentions Chanukah and it may have been kept by early Christians. But there are very real differences between Christmas and Chanukah. Chanukah is about the birth of a whole community, a new beginning for Judaism and a religious dedication renewed each year.

Passover
Lynne Scholefield

Contents

Introduction

Imagine a smell or the taste of certain foods which bring back memories. It might be fresh-baked bread or newly-ground coffee or a turkey roasting in the oven.

Every year in a Jewish home the sight, smell and taste of certain foods bring back memories of a story. It is a story of freedom and Jews relive it every spring. Spring is the time of year for thinking about new life and for being joyful about it.

Passover (or Pesach as it is more accurately called) is all about new life — new life for a whole people, the Jews; new life for a country, Israel; and a new way of life for individual Jews all over the world. This new way of life is based on the Jewish law, the Torah.

1

The Celebrations

In every country where Jews live there are slightly different customs at festival times. This book is about the way Passover might be celebrated in a Jewish home in Britain. The Jewish calendar is different from the calendar most people in Britain follow but Passover usually takes place around April, in the Jewish month of Nisan.

Preparations begin with the house being cleaned and any leaven removed. (Leaven is any substance which will make dough rise, such as yeast or self-raising flour.) Passover is also called the Feast of Unleavened Bread and during the eight days that it lasts no leaven ('chametz' is the Hebrew word) is allowed in the house.

To make sure that the house is free of chametz a search takes place on the evening before the festival begins. This is done with great care and ceremony. A candle is used for a light. Any piece of chametz which is found is swept up, usually with a feather, and is burnt the following morning. Sometimes one of the children will hide some small pieces of chametz and the search becomes the first of the Passover games involving all the family.

Before the game starts a blessing is said, usually by the father. This is a kind of prayer. It is quite short and is spoken in Hebrew. One of the blessings used most often in Judaism is:

Baruch ata Adōnoy, Elōhaynu melech ha-ōlom,
bōray pree ha-gafen.

Blessed are you, Lord our God, King of the
Universe who brings forth fruit from the vine.

Nearly every activity during Passover begins with a blessing. This is because the festival is a religious celebration. But it takes place at home, not in the synagogue, the Jewish place of worship. Nevertheless it follows carefully all the details in the Torah.

Judaism is all about following the Torah, the first five books of what Christians call the Old Testament; they are Genesis, Exodus, Leviticus, Numbers and Deuteronomy. The Book of Exodus tells the story of Moses and how he led the Israelites out of slavery and towards the Promised Land. It also contains many of the laws of God, including the Ten Commandments.

All the laws of the Torah show how God wants his people to live. They tell them how they should treat one another and, above all, how they should love God.

Every Jewish child knows the Shema. The words tell us what it means to be a Jew. They are recited every day in Hebrew. In English it reads:

Hear, O Israel, the Lord our God, the Lord is One, and you
shall love the Lord your God with all your heart and with all
your soul and with all your might.

Passover celebrates the way in which God freed the Jews from slavery in Egypt, led them to their own land and gave them the law through Moses so that the people would know how to love and worship him. Every year when children ask why they are looking for leaven or eating special foods, parents have a chance to retell the story. This has been happening for over three thousand years.

There are synagogue services to celebrate Passover but the Seder meal on the first or second evening of the festival takes place at home. It always follows a set order. This order is written down in a book called the Haggadah. 'Haggadah' means simply 'telling' or 'story'. The book contains all the words for the proper ordering of the meal which is a religious service. The Haggadah itself is always on the table with the other items.

Throughout the Seder meal many different things are going on. No one gets bored or forgotten. There are prayers, special things to eat from the Seder plate, questions for the youngest child to ask, a huge meal to be eaten, wine to drink, stories and singing.

Father reads from the Haggadah

The candles on the table are lit. The wine is poured out and a glassful is drunk for the first time while the blessing is said (wine is drunk at four different times during the Seder). Then Father breaks the matzo (the special unleavened bread) and passes a piece to everyone. Then each person reaches out and takes a small selection of green vegetables, usually parsley or lettuce, dips it in salt water and eats it.

At this point in the meal the 'four questions' are asked. The

Ancient Haggadah

Passover

youngest child present stands up and asks why everything is different on Passover night. He asks:

1 'Why do we have unleavened bread?'
2 'Why do we eat bitter herbs?'
3 'Why do we dip our herbs in salt water?'
4 'Why do we sit in a reclining position on cushions?'

Usually these questions are asked in Hebrew. Sometimes they are sung, either by the child on his own or with help from the other members of the family.

MA NISHTANA

Ma nish-ta-na ha-lai-lah ha-zeh mi-kol ha-lei - lot, mi-

- kol ha-lei - lot? She-b' - hol ha-lei-lot a - nu oh-lin 1.ha-
2.sh' -

- meitz __ u - ma-tzah, ha - meitz __ u - ma-tzah. Ha-
- ar ____ y' - ra - kot, sh' - ar ____ y' - ra kot. Ha-

- lai - lah ha-zeh, ha - lai-lah ha-zeh ku-lo __ ma - tzah, __ ha-
- lai - lah ha-zeh, ha - lai-lah ha-zeh ku-lo __ ma - ror, ____ ha-

- lai - lah ha-zeh ha - lai-lah ha-zeh ku-lo __ ma - tzah. 2.She-b'-
- lai - lah ha-zeh ha - lai-lah ha-zeh ku-lo __ ma - ror.

3. She-b'-hol ha-lei-lot ein a-nu mat-bi-lin a-fi-lu pa-am e-hat.
   Ha-lai-lah ha-zeh, ha-lai-lah ha-zeh sh'-tei f'a-a-mim.

4. She-b'-hol ha-lei-lot a-nu oh-lin bein yosh-vin u-vein m'-su-bin.
   Ha-lai-lah ha-zeh, ha-lai-lah ha-zeh ku-la-nu m'-su-bin.

It is the father of the family who has to reply. He begins to tell the story of how God brought the Israelites out of slavery in Egypt into the freedom of the Promised Land.

While he speaks he points to the foods on the Seder dish. At the appropriate places in the story the bitter herbs are eaten, with a piece of matzo and sometimes with the sweet, sticky charoset.

After the main meal has been eaten, more prayers are said and the third and fourth glasses of wine are drunk. The Seder ends with singing. This usually consists of folk-songs which tell the Passover story in another way.

The story, which has been handed down for thousands of years and which Passover still celebrates, is told in detail in the next chapter.

DAYEINU

I - lu ho-tzi ho-tzi-a-nu, ho-tzi-a-nu mi-mitz-ra-yim,
ho-tzi-a-nu mi-mitz-ra-yim da-yei-nu.
Chorus
Da-da-yei-nu,___ da-da-yei-nu,___ da-da-yei-nu, da-
1,2: -yei-nu da-yei-nu da-yei-nu.
3: yei-nu da-yei-nu.

2. I-lu na-tan, na-tan la-nu, na-tan la-nu et ha-sha-bat, na-tan la-nu
   et ha-sha-bat, dayeinu. (Chorus).

3. I-lu na-tan, na-tan la-nu, na-tan la-nu et ha-to-rah, na-tan la-nu et
   ha-to-rah, dayeinu. (Chorus).

2

The Story

This is the way in which the telling of the Passover story begins:

> Youngest child: *'Why is this night different from all other nights?'*
> Father: (uncovers matzos) *'We were slaves to Pharaoh in Egypt and the Lord our God brought us out from there with a strong hand and an outstretched arm. . .'*

The story is set out in the Haggadah (the 'telling') and is usually told by the eldest male Jew present at the Seder. It includes the details which are in the Book of Exodus along with the comments and teachings of various rabbis. These are the teachers who through the centuries have tried to deepen the Jewish understanding of history and the way it is related to the present.

> Father: *'If God had not brought out our forefathers, then Jews today and in the future might still have been slaves. The story of our departure is well worth telling and so each year our children ask about it and learn the way God freed us from Egypt.*
> *'The Torah speaks about four sons who ask the questions in different ways. The first son is wise and asks about the*

meaning of laws which God has given us. *We can explain all the details of Pesach to him. The wicked son says, "What is the meaning of the service to* you?" *He excludes himself from the Seder and so really he excludes himself from the freedom too. The simple son asks, "What is this?" and you can give him a simple answer: "With a strong hand God brought us out of Egypt, from slavery". For the son who can't even ask a question you must still tell him that Pesach celebrates how God freed us from Egypt.'*

Us not *them.*\Try to imagine that you are reliving that night when the Jews left Egypt.

'We hadn't always been there. God chose Abraham and made a covenant with him. He had to leave his home and the idol worship behind, and God made him the father of a new nation. He had a son, Isaac, and two grandsons, Jacob and Esau. One of Jacob's sons was Joseph and it was he who brought the whole family to Egypt. God had told Abraham that there would be a time of slavery and oppression but that they would come through it. They would be saved. He was right, but it didn't happen only once. There have been many times of oppression and the need for salvation (here the speaker raises his cup of wine).

'In Egypt the Jews grew in numbers and perhaps that frightened the Egyptians; they thought we might fight against them. They made us slaves and forced us to do their labouring and building. But that wasn't enough for the Pharaoh. He ordered that every new-born baby boy was to be thrown into the River Nile. When Moses was born his parents hid him and then made a floating crib so he wouldn't drown in the river. He was found by the Pharaoh's daughter and was brought up by her as an Egyptian prince.

'Years later Moses saw what was happening to his own people and he killed a cruel Egyptian. He was forced to leave, but returned to Egypt after many years for God had promised

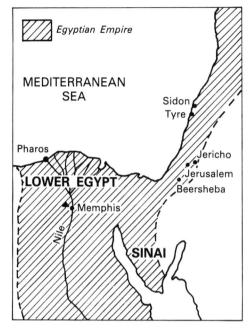

Present-day Israel

Passover

that he would bring his people out with a strong arm and with signs and wonders. There were the plagues, the Angel of Death, the journey through the desert, and the law given to Moses on Mount Sinai.

'Moses confronted Pharaoh, asking him to release the Jewish slaves but the king wouldn't give up his workforce. Then strange things started to happen. First there was the plague of blood, then frogs. They only affected the Egyptians. God had made a division, so in Goshan, where Jews lived, there were no frogs or anything else. Each time, Pharaoh gave way and said we could go, and then when the plague stopped he said we couldn't. In the end there was a final, terrible plague. The first-born of every Egyptian household was to die.

A drop of wine is spilled for each plague
BLOOD
FROGS
LICE
WILD BEASTS
BLIGHT
BOILS
HAIL
LOCUSTS
DARKNESS
DEATH OF THE FIRST BORN

'Moses gave instructions for us to kill a lamb and put some of the blood around the door. "When the Angel of Death comes," said Moses, "he will see the blood and pass over the house." And so it was. In every Egyptian house someone died. The Egyptians were terrified and urged Moses to take the Jews away as fast as possible.

'*Following Moses' instructions everyone had packed their things and had eaten a special meal the night before — some of the lamb, unleavened bread and bitter herbs. Early in the morning with that day's bread still unrisen we left.*'

THE EXODUS

Therefore let us rejoice
At the wonder of our deliverance,
From bondage to freedom,
From agony to joy,
From mourning to festivity,
From darkness to light,
From slavery to redemption
Before God let us sing a new song.

(words from the Haggadah)

That is the end of the Passover story but it is not the end of the story of freedom. Moses led the Jews safely across the Red Sea (the Egyptian pursuers were drowned) and into the desert. There were many more problems and many more miracles before the Promised Land was reached. That itself is the beginning of another story which is still continuing. In the desert, at Sinai, Moses received the Torah and a new covenant was made between God and his chosen people, an agreement that is renewed every year at Passover.

The Seder meal ends with these words:

'*The redemption is not yet complete. . .*
Peace, shalom. . .
Next year in Jerusalem,
Next year may all be free.'

3

The Passover Symbols

Many of the objects and activities which occur in the Seder seem to be there so that someone will ask, 'Why?' The order of the meal gives every opportunity for probing further and further into the meanings behind what is being done.

Some of the answers to the questions are written in the Haggadah. When the youngest child asks the 'four questions' the story is told in great detail. The meaning of each of the special foods is explained. The reason for drinking wine on four different occasions is given.

But as well as all these traditional answers each individual family will have other, more personal meanings to give. There may be in the family more recent examples of freedom. Some of these may be about the dreadful time before and during the Second World War when many Jewish families suffered persecution in Europe. A few survived or escaped and found new freedom in Israel and other countries. The word 'Exodus' was often used again at that time. Today many Jews are trying to escape to freedom from other parts of the world. So at Passover time, especially, Jews think and talk about these things and the hope for peace in the future.

For all this the basic symbols remain the same. Passover is also the Feast of Unleavened Bread. It lasts for seven or eight days and during this time no leavened bread is eaten, only

Jewish immigrants arrested while illegally attempting to enter Israel in 1947

matzo. During the Seder the question is always asked, 'Why do we eat matzos?' The answer is always the same:

> 'We eat matzos because we had to leave Egypt in a hurry. There wasn't time to bake bread with yeast in. We ate the unleavened bread with the roasted lamb and the bitter herbs. We were packed and dressed for the journey, ready to go at midnight.'

Notice how always Jews refer to their ancestors as 'we'. 'We eat matzos.' 'We had to leave Egypt in a hurry.' It is this real sense of belonging which is at the heart of everything which Jews believe and do. Passover is, in every way, a family celebration. A Jew feels related to every other Jew in the world and to every other Jew in history.

Jews in the former Soviet Union faced many restrictions. Here Jewish women are buying matzos despite the possibility of arrest.

In giving his answer to the 'four questions' the Jewish father refers to the items on the Seder plate.

Lamb bone   Usually the shank bone of a lamb is used. This is a reminder of the lamb which was killed so that its blood could be painted on the doorposts and lintels of the slaves' huts in Egypt. It was the sign that the Angel of Death should *'pass over'*. It has also become a symbol of the strong arm of God taking care of his people, the Jews.

Egg   The egg is usually hard boiled and then 'roasted' in a flame for a few seconds. It is a symbol of new life. In some countries a hard-boiled egg forms the first course of the Passover meal.

Jewish families in some Eastern European countries keep up a tradition of painting the shells of these eggs with different patterns and colours. Sometimes one of the eggs is left

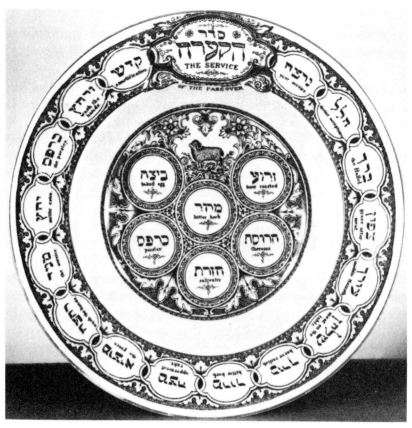

Seder dish

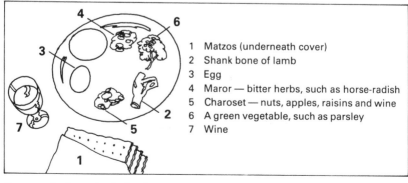

1 Matzos (underneath cover)
2 Shank bone of lamb
3 Egg
4 Maror — bitter herbs, such as horse-radish
5 Charoset — nuts, apples, raisins and wine
6 A green vegetable, such as parsley
7 Wine

Passover foods on the Seder dish

Passover

unboiled. Any child in the family who knows how that one is painted can have great fun playing tricks on other members of the family!

Green vegetable (karpas)   This is usually parsley or lettuce. It is a symbol of life and the way in which God provided for the Israelites in the wilderness, giving them food and water. At springtime it is also a reminder of the green fields — of the fact that growth has begun again and life goes on.

Bitter herbs (maror)   This is usually horse-radish, which has a bitter taste. It is intended to be a symbol of slavery. If it brings tears to your eyes so much the better. That will remind you that being a slave is always a terrible and bitter thing.

Charoset   This is a mixture of fruit, nuts, spices and wine. In contrast with the bitter herbs this mixture tastes sweet and pleasant. It is a symbol of the taste of freedom, which is always sweet. Some Jews also suggest that the brown, sticky mixture is a reminder of the mortar with which the slaves in Egypt had to make bricks.

CHAROSET

**4 tablespoons chopped nuts
(walnuts, hazelnuts or almonds)
1 small cooking apple, grated
1 teaspoon cinnamon
a little wine**

Mix all the ingredients together and bind into a paste with the wine. Form into a flat round shape and serve on the Seder Dish.

Salt water   Also on the Seder table is a bowl of salt water. The karpas is dipped into this during the Seder, as are the eggs if they are eaten as part of the meal. This represents the tears of pain and sorrow shed by the slaves before they were freed.

Wine   During the meal wine is drunk at four different times. This is a reminder of the fourfold promise which God gave to Moses. It can be found in the Book of Exodus 6: 6–8. God promised that he would: (1) deliver them from slavery; (2) redeem them; (3) take them as his chosen people; (4) give them a land of their own.

4

Details of the Seder

Passover is not just a reminder of a story. In the past it was closely linked with agriculture and the spring, and it is also called the Feast of Unleavened Bread. The search for chametz is the climax of preparations to remove all leaven from the house. This begins with spring-cleaning when all leavened items are collected together and 'sold' to a non-Jew who keeps them during the festival. Afterwards they can be bought back. In many Jewish homes the ordinary crockery, cutlery, and cooking equipment are packed away and a special Passover set is used for the eight days.

These rules about food are called 'making things kosher'. This means 'fit' or 'right'. Many packaged goods carry the words 'kosher for Passover'. The basis for the rules can be found in the Torah. Exodus 13: 6–7 gives the Passover details.

This passage goes on to tell fathers that they must pass on the story to their sons. The Seder is the annual opportunity to do so. Everyone comes together at home in the family setting, often three generations together, to explain and learn what it is all about. Friends may be there too, especially if they are poor and cannot afford their own Seder. The order is flexible to take account of different needs, but during the meal there are several details which appeal especially to children.

When the middle matzo is broken at the beginning of the Seder one part is put aside and covered. It is the 'afikomen' — a Greek word meaning 'afterwards'. It is eaten at the end of the

A Jewish family at the Seder

meal and the Seder cannot be completed until it is eaten. The leader often hides the afikomen and the children have to find it. It is so important that the one who does discover it may claim a reward, either money or a present. It is then returned and is the last food tasted.

Also intriguing is the presence of Elijah's cup on the table. Elijah was a prophet in the Old Testament and there is a legend that he returns to earth dressed as a beggar to see whether people will receive him. Towards the end of the Seder a child is sent to open the door so that Elijah will know he is welcome. A cup of wine is waiting for him too. The Jews hope that one day God will complete the work of freedom begun in

Egypt by sending a specially chosen Messiah. Other prophets in the Old Testament said that Elijah would come first to prepare the people. There is a tradition that if every Jew faithfully kept just one Sabbath the Messiah would come. The leader of the Seder says:

> 'Elijah opens up for us the realm of mystery and wonder;
> Let us now open the door for Elijah.'

After the meal the family does not leave the table. Instead they sing songs together mainly about Passover. Many of these folk-songs have words and phrases repeated again and again so even very young children can learn them. Probably the best known is called *Only one kid.*

HAD GADYA

One little goat, one little goat,
   My father bought for two zuzim.
One little goat, one little goat.

Then came a cat and ate the goat
   My father bought for two zuzim.
One little goat, one little goat.

Then came a dog and bit the cat,
   That ate the goat
My father bought for two zuzim.
   One little goat, one little goat.

Then came a stick and beat the dog,
   That bit the cat that ate the goat
My father bought for two zuzim.
   One little goat, one little goat.

Then came a fire and burned the stick,
   That beat the dog that bit the cat
That ate the goat
   My father bought for two zuzim.
One little goat, one little goat.

                                                Passover

Then came the water and quenched the fire,
   That burned the stick that beat the dog
That bit the cat that ate the goat
   My father bought for two zuzim.
One little goat, one little goat.

Then came an ox and drank the water,
   That quenched the fire that burned the stick
That beat the dog that bit the cat
   That ate the goat
My father bought for two zuzim.
   One little goat, one little goat.

Then came a *shohet* and slaughtered the ox,
   That drank the water that quenched the fire
That burned the stick that beat the dog
   That bit the cat that ate the goat
My father bought for two zuzim.
   One little goat, one little goat.

Then came the angel of death and killed the *shohet,*
   That slaughtered the ox that drank the water
That quenched the fire that burned the stick
   That beat the dog that bit the cat
That ate the goat
   My father bought for two zuzim.
One little goat, one little goat.

Then came the Holy One, blessed be He,
   And slew the angel of death,
That killed the *shohet* that slaughtered the ox
   That drank the water that quenched the fire
That burned the stick that beat the dog
   That bit the cat that ate the goat
My father bought for two zuzim.
   One little goat, one little goat.

The singing can be enjoyed by everyone but at other times the words and ideas are more for the adults present. Each year something new may be understood about the salvation story. When the leader breaks the middle matzo he says:

'This is the bread of affliction'

Affliction means suffering, being in trouble, and Jewish families were not only 'in affliction' in Egypt. The story of Judaism is often one of oppression and persecution. Six million Jews died in Europe during the Second World War when Nazi leaders tried to kill every single Jew through the use of concentration and extermination camps. In many Jewish families there are no grandparents or uncles and aunts alive. In the 1930s and 1940s, when Passover was celebrated, Jews were tasting the bread of affliction in a very real way. When they said 'Now we are all still slaves. Next year may all be free', they knew that freedom would be very sweet indeed.

The Holocaust Museum, Jerusalem

This is the bread of affliction,
the poor bread,
which our fathers ate in the land
of Egypt.
Let all who are hungry come and eat.
Let all who are in want
share the hope of Passover.
As we celebrate here
we join with people everywhere.
This year we celebrate here.
Next year in the land of Israel.
Now we are still slaves.
Next year may all be free.

Freedom for the Jews has always been associated with Israel, the Promised Land, and each Passover ends with the words:

Next year in Jerusalem!
Next year may all be free!

The Western Wall, Jerusalem

In 70 C.E. the Jews were finally beaten by the Romans. Jerusalem, the symbol of Israel, was destroyed. For nearly nineteen hundred years there was a belief that one day the Jews would return to Israel. 'Next year in Jerusalem,' they said, and, indeed, following the Second World War, Israel once again became the Jewish homeland. The State of Israel was officially recognized in 1948.

Passover, then, can never simply be a happy occasion. There is too much of the dark side to the story. One rabbi taught that when the Egyptian armies were drowning in the sea the heavenly hosts broke out in songs of jubilation. God silenced them and said, 'My creatures are perishing, and you sing praises?' When the plagues are mentioned a drop of wine is spilled for each one — the cup of joy is lessened by the suffering of the Egyptians and they are remembered.

This is all in the past. What does Passover look forward to? The final words of the Seder sum this up:

> *Peace, Shalom*
> *Peace for us! For everyone!*
> *For all people, this, our hope:*
> *Next year in Jerusalem!*
> *Next year may all be free!*

THINGS TO DO

Rosh Hashanah and Yom Kippur

1 Card making. People always send one another Rosh Hashanah or New Year cards. You can design and make your own, using lots of different techniques. Use this book for ideas and pictures. Obvious subjects are the shofar, the fruits, or some of the Bible stories, such as Jonah. Jewish New Year cards can also be bought to help you with ideas.

2 Blowing the shofar. Rams' horns are not easy to come by nowadays, although they can still be bought for a price. If you visit a synagogue you will almost certainly be shown one and may be allowed to try blowing it. The shofar has a mouthpiece like a trumpet's and is blown like one. The mouthpiece is placed against the right corner of the mouth and the air pushed between the lips. The three basic calls (tekiah, shevarim and teruah) are described in the book. You can, in fact, play different notes on the shofar with practice, as you can on a bugle. Someone who can blow the shofar well is called a Ba'al Tekiah. It is great fun, but very noisy!

3 The Vidui or 'Confession'. Write out the alphabet and make your own list of sins that need repentance. For example:
We have been <u>a</u>ngry.
We have <u>b</u>lamed others unfairly.
We have <u>c</u>aused our parents to worry unnecessarily.

4 Making a honey cake. Honey cake is traditionally eaten at Rosh Hashanah. Here is a recipe to make.

½ jar clear honey (225 g)	½ tsp ground ginger
2 large eggs	½ tsp cinnamon
100g caster sugar	½ tsp mixed spice
3 tbsp vegetable oil	½ tsp bicarbonate of soda
200g self-raising flour	150ml warm water

Grease and line cake tin. Beat eggs and sugar together. Stir in oil and honey. Mix flour and spices together. Add bicarbonate of soda to the water and add to egg mixture alternately with flour until you have a smooth, fairly thick mixture. Pour into cake tin and bake in centre of moderate oven (160°C, 320°F, Gas Mark 3) for about 75 minutes. Let the cake cool for 5 minutes, then turn out of the tin and leave until cold.

5 Tsedakah – giving charity. Find a way in which you, as a class, can help somebody else. Look at all the charities which need help. You may have to find ways of raising money, such as sponsored walks or jumble sales. If you can have some contact with the person(s) you are helping, perhaps by correspondence if they are in another country, that will make it more real. Perhaps it might be a good idea to help with something you take for granted or even think you dislike – helping someone to go to school and get an education, for example. You can decide for yourselves the best way to practise tsedakah.

Succot and Simchat Torah

1 Write out these words and explain what they mean:

succah   etrog   lulav   synagogue
Torah   Shabbat   pilgrimage   Talmud

2 Try to answer these questions:

(a) Why is the lulav not waved on Shabbat?

(b) One of the Ten Commandments forbids murder. What do you think counts as murder?

(c) Briefly describe at least two events in your life, or your family's life, you have celebrated.

3 The first word in the Torah is בְּרֵאשִׁית , 'breshit'. It means 'in the beginning'. Copy the Hebrew letters and colour them. Do the same for the last word in the Torah: יִשְׂרָאֵל , 'Israel'.

4 Make a model of a succah out of a cardboard box. Decorate it with pictures of fruit and vegetables cut out of magazines and weave a roof from leafy twigs or grasses.

5 (a) Draw a Simchat Torah flag. The star and border are blue and the background is white.

(b) Find out about the different ways in which the Star of David has been and is being used. (*Clues:* during the Holocaust; in synagogues.)

6 Design a poster to decorate a succah. You could use Hebrew words or drawings of harvest produce.

7 Make a diagram to show your own journey through life. Mark on it all the important events so far. Add your hopes and fears for the future.

8 The words of Ecclesiastes 3:1–8 have been set to music in a song called 'Turn, Turn, Turn' by Pete Seeger. Listen to a recording of the song and sing it yourselves. Then make a wallchart showing the aspects of life the words refer to. Discuss in small groups whether you agree with the words or not.

9 Express your ideas about the theme of 'celebration' in a painting, a drawing, a story or a poem.

10 Try some Jewish cookery. Find a Jewish cookery book and experiment, or use one of the recipes below. Stuffed cabbage is a traditional Succot dish, and apple candy makes a good harvest treat.

APPLE CANDY

8 apples   sugar   rosewater

Cut the apples into quarters and core but do not peel. Place them in a saucepan. Cover with a little water and bring to the boil. Reduce the heat and simmer the apples until very soft. Blend them in a blender or put them through a sieve.

Use one cup of sugar for each cup of apple pulp. Bring the sugar and apple pulp to the boil, lower the heat and simmer for an hour, stirring every few minutes. When the consistency is like very thick jam, add the rosewater and pour the mixture into a baking tin about 20 cm square, sprinkled with sugar.

Allow the candy to cool. Cut into squares and sprinkle with more sugar. Let the candy dry at room temperature for a few days. The same method can be used for peaches or pears.

STUFFED CABBAGE

12 large cabbage leaves	1 450-gram tin peeled tomatoes
500 grams minced meat	2 tablespoons sugar
50 grams long-grain rice	1 teaspoon lemon juice
2 large onions, finely chopped	½ teaspoon salt
1 large carrot, grated	stock

Wash the cabbage leaves and pour boiling water over them to blanch them. Cut out the hard stalks. Wash the rice, then mix it with the meat and half the chopped onion. Put some of the meat mixture on each leaf and roll up like a parcel. Using a large pan, fry the rest of the onion and the grated carrot in the oil for a few minutes. Add the cabbage rolls to the pan and pour in enough stock to cover them. Add the salt, sugar, lemon juice and tomatoes. Cook for about 3 hours in a medium oven, preferably in a casserole dish with a tightly fitting lid.

Things to Do

Chanukah

1 Make a Chanukah menorah or candlestick. If you are going to put real candles in it and light them, make sure that it has a good solid base so that it cannot fall over. Make sure that it is not made out of material which will easily catch fire. Modelling clay will do.
2 Write out the blessing said by the Jewish father at the lighting of the first candle. Learn it by heart.
3 Write down the following Hebrew words and put their English meanings alongside. If you can, also write some of them in Hebrew script:

> menorah
> shamash
> *Shehechiyanu*
> Chanukiyah
> svivon
> Shema
> Chanukah
> Torah

4 Learn the festival song *Ma'oz Tzur* and sing it as a group in class.
5 Make a dreidel using the following instructions and play one of the games described in the text.

a *Cut a square out of a piece of stiff card.*

b *Pierce the centre of the square and push a matchstick through the hole.*

c *On each side of the square mark the following letters in Hebrew script: Nun* **ב** *Gimmel* **ג** *Heh* **ה** *Shin* **שׁ**

Your dreidel is now ready to be spun. Can you make up a game of your own?

נֵס גָּדוֹל הָיָה שָׁם

6 Write out in both Hebrew and English the words 'A Great Miracle Happened Here'. Remember that Hebrew is written from right to left.

7 From an encyclopedia find out all you can about Antiochus Epiphanes.

8 Collect together the ingredients and make some Latkes using the following recipe:
Ingredients for 4-6 people

RECIPE

6 medium-sized potatoes   *1 onion (optional)*
2 eggs   *50g of flour*
1 teaspoon of salt   *Vegetable oil or fat for frying*

Directions: Peel the potatoes and soak in cold water for half an hour. Grate the potatoes and drain off the excess liquid. Peel and grate the onion into the potatoes. Beat the eggs and add them to the mixture together with the flour and salt. Stir to make a smooth batter. Heat the fat in a heavy pan. Drop the batter from a spoon into the hot fat, making one large or several small pancakes. Fry until brown, then turn to brown other side. Lift out and drain off fat. Serve with grated cheese.

---

9 Read the story of Nebuchadnezzar in the Book of Daniel, Chapter 3. This story was written down at the time of the Maccabean revolt. Retell it as you imagine a story-teller would have told it to the freedom fighters gathered round a fire in the hills above Jerusalem at night. Do the same with the story in Daniel, Chapter 6, also first written down at that time. Why do you think stories like these suddenly became important for the Jews?

Things to Do

10 Retell the stories of Hannah and Mattathias as you think an eyewitness might have told them.
11 Tell the story of the Maccabean revolt for very young children. Make a booklet and include pictures.
12 Imagine you are one of the Maccabees living in the hills and joining in the raiding parties on the troops of Antiochus. Write a letter home to your family describing the type of life you lead and your feelings.
13 Describe the entry of Judas Maccabeus into Jerusalem.
14 Find a recording of the piece of music *Judas Maccabaeus* by Handel. Play it and discuss what the music conveys.
15 Using the title 'The Light in the Darkness', design a drawing, a painting, a stained-glass window; or write a piece of music, a song, a play or a mime.
16 Design a Chanukah board game which can be played with a group of people. Include the events in the story and the way the festival is celebrated nowadays.
17 Prepare a Chanukah crossword where every clue and each answer is about the festival.
18 Act a Chanukah play. Divide the story up into sections and let a different group write each one. Present the performances, one group after another, to the rest of the class.
19 Read the story as it is written in the Books of Maccabees. The main story is in 1 Maccabees 1:41–4:61 and in 2 Maccabees 4:7–7:42. You will probably need the help of your teacher to find the books, which are in a collection Christians call the Apochrypha. Sometimes the Apochrypha is included in Bibles but usually it has to be bought separately.
20 Why do you think the miracle of the oil was important just at the time it happened? Are symbols sometimes as important as events?

Passover

1 Copy out the Shema and learn to recite it (see page 76).
2 Learn one of the songs associated with Passover and sing it.
3 Choose a title such as 'Freedom', 'Past and Present', or 'Celebration' and make a collage, or a drawing, or write a poem or story. You could make use of the Passover story or you could use other incidents from Jewish history.
4 Look up the Ten Commandments in Exodus 20: 1–17. These are part of the Torah. Discuss what they mean and the sort of attitudes and behaviour which they encourage.
5 Make a strip cartoon of the Passover story. You could do this individually or as a group doing one picture each and mounting them in order.
6 Make a display about Israel today, its history, places and people.
7 Try to answer these question as fully as you can:
  (a) Where does the name 'Passover' come from?
  (b) Which country is specially associated with the Jews?
  (c) What are the symbols used in the Seder to represent
      (i) new life
      (ii) bitterness of slavery
      (iii) sweet taste of freedom
  (d) Why is unleavened bread (matzo) eaten during Passover?
  (e) What is a blessing? Why are so many used in Jewish life?
  (f) Why do you think Jewish families go on remembering something which happened so long ago?

BOOKS AND OTHER RESOURCES

Books

Barnett, V. *A Jewish Family in Britain*. Families and Faiths Series, RMEP, 1984.

Bryan, C. and Whitburn, V. *Shabbat*. Living Festivals Series, RMEP, 1984.

Forta, A. *Judaism*. Examining Religions Series, Heinemann, 1989.

Holm, J. *Growing Up in Judaism*. Longman, 1990.

Jacobs, L. *The Book of Jewish Practice*. Behrman House Inc., 1987.

Lawton, C. *I Am a Jew*. Franklin Watts, 1984.

————. *Judaism*. Religion through Festivals Series, Longman, 1989.

Mayled, J. *Jewish Festivals Teacher's Book*. Living Festivals Series, RMEP, 1988.

Pilkington, C. M. *Judaism: An Approach for GCSE*. Hodder & Stoughton, 1991.

Rudge, J., Read, G. and Teece, G. *Jews. Books 1–4*. The Westhill Project, Stanley Thornes, 1990/91.

————. *Judaism: Teacher's Manual*. The Westhill Project, Stanley Thornes, 1990.

Thorley, S. *Judaism in Words and Pictures*. RMEP, 1992 (updated edition).

Turner, R. *Jewish Festivals*. Wayland, 1985.

Videos

Aspects of Judaism. Exmouth School World Religions Series, Videotext. Available from RMEP.

Believe It or Not Series. Video 2 includes Passover; Video 6 includes Succot. Central TV. Also available from RMEP.

The Jewish Festival of Passover. ILEA Video. Available from Educational Media, 235 Imperial Drive, Rayners Lane, Harrow, Middx HA3 7HE.

Living Festivals Videos. Video 1 includes Chanukah and Passover; Video 2 includes Succot. CEM Video. Also available from RMEP.

Other Audio-visual Aids

Jewish Festivals (4 posters plus notes; ref. E.746). PCET, 27 Kirchen Road, London W13 0UD.

Jews Photopack (20 photographs plus notes). The Westhill Project, Stanley Thornes.

Judaism (6 posters plus notes). CEM, Royal Buildings, Victoria Street, Derby DE13 1GW.

Passover (tape-slide pack). Westhill RE Centre. Available from Stanley Thornes.

Useful addresses

Jewish Education Bureau
8 Westcombe Avenue
Leeds LS8 2BS

Council of Christians and Jews
48 Onslow Gardens
London SW7 3PX